"Dr. Nancy Buck presents a clear, comprehensive process to help parents develop and maintain the vital relationship necessary for a healthy future f⌐⌐ ⌐⌐ ⌐⌐ ⌐⌐ ⌐ation. *Peaceful Parenting* is a ⌐⌐ ⌐⌐ ng the issue of parenting, an ⌐⌐ ⌐h approach. Read this book ⌐⌐ ⌐ how what Nancy does teach ⌐⌐ ⌐e responsibility for what the⌐

From the forward by
Dr. William Glasser

"The style of writing is as gentle and patient as the approach recommended. The theory is convincing and manifests common sense. The multiple anecdotes and examples are offered all in good humor and humility. I mean it sincerely when I say that this book needs to be widely available to today's parents, teachers, and all others who are involved in the loving and responsible nurturing of children. I say this as a clergyperson, a father and a grandfather."

Dr. William Houff
Unitarian Universalist Minister

"Dr. Buck speaks directly to parents who seek to engage in child rearing practices that are neither overly permissive nor harshly punitive. The readily accessible writing style, free of jargon and rich in concrete examples, is ideally suited to parents. Particularly impressive is the perspective of "peaceful" which emphasizes cooperation and constructive competitiveness. This emphasis contrasts with the negativity and retribution of such approaches as "tough love parenting."

Dr. Mary Sheerin
Early Childhood Specialist

"The use of choice theory is not only sound, it obviously works! Also, the stories enrich the theory in chapter after chapter. This book will be warmly welcomed and read cover-to-cover by parents and those who are "expecting" to be parents. It has practical application across the child/adolescent life span. I encourage all to read this important book."

Dr. Gail Brophy
Academic Dean
The Union Institute

Peaceful Parenting

By

Nancy S. Buck, Ph.D.

Peaceful Parenting
PO Box 271
Portsmouth RI 02871
www.peacefulparenting.com

BLACK FOREST PRESS
San Diego, California
May 2000
First Edition

Peaceful Parenting
PO Box 271
Portsmouth NH 03802
www.peacefulparenting.com

Peaceful Parenting

By

Nancy S. Buck, Ph.D.

PUBLISHED IN THE UNITED STATES OF AMERICA
BY
BLACK FOREST PRESS
P.O.Box 6342
Chula Vista, CA 91909-6342
1-800-451-9404

To terry
may your home be filled with peace,
joy and laughter
                    Nancy A Buck

Cover Design by
Penni and Dale Neely

Disclaimer

Printed in the United States of America
Library of Congress
Cataloging-in-Publication

ISBN:1-58275-014-9

Table of Contents

Table of Contents
For Tables

FOREWORD

Peaceful Parenting is a desperately needed book. News headlines inform us of the increasing self-destructive activity of our young people including the incomprehensible acts of children shooting other children. What can be done to stop the flood of what seems to be our youth out of control? Two important research studies indicate that improving and maintaining a child's connection with his parents and helping parents improve their parenting skills makes a significant difference in keeping youth on a healthy path of becoming responsible, contributing adults. (See footnote) Dr. Nancy Buck presents a clear, comprehensive process to help parents develop and maintain the vital relationship necessary for a healthy future for our families and our nation. As an associate of mine for over 20 years, she has combined her experiences as a Senior Faculty member of The William Glasser Institute and her own personal experience as a parent to write a book specifically addressing the issue of effective parenting, an area that very much needs a fresh approach.

The two most important things we do in our lives, for which we have little or no preparation, are getting married and raising children. When a parent has difficulty with a child, the parent will often fall back on his or her parent's behaviors, many of which did not work then and have little or no chance of working now. The vast majority of family unhappiness is the result of well-intentioned parents trying to make children do what they don't want to do. In search of freedom, children resist their parent's effort. This book teaches parents how to love their children without controlling them. Using these ideas, parents will learn how to have a loving relationship with their child that will last a lifetime. Parents will learn how to help their child learn how to satisfy his or her need for love without believing he or she has to satisfy anyone else's conditions to get that love.

What Nancy teaches in this book is not so much a series of dos and don'ts that rarely fit the situation for which they are intended. Instead she will teach you the choice theory that explains the source of the child's behavior and then how to figure out a choice theory behavior that has the best chance of working in that particular situation. As you use the choice theory, you begin to see not only what works but, also, how it works so you can use it in a similar situation.

The biggest concern of most parents is the future of their children: Will they lead happy and successful lives. What is equally important is: Will they like to spend time with me and me with them? If the children are happy and like spending time with the parents, the parents are well satisfied. The most critical choice a parent can make throughout their child's life is to not choose to do anything with a child whom you want to grow up to be happy, successful and close to you, that you believe will increase the distance between you. Some parents may be asking, "Are we suppose to abdicate our responsibility as parents? Let our children do anything they want?" That is hardly what I am saying. Learning choice theory helps parents better understand their child, themselves, and how to make choices that will keep you connected with one another as you teach your child to be responsible for him or herself.

Learning choice theory is not difficult. But it is difficult to put into practice because in almost every instance what it teaches goes against the common sense you have been learning and using since birth. It is that faulty common sense, I call it external control psychology, that you will learn to replace with the much more effective choice theory. Believing we know what's right for our children, most parents reward and punish in an attempt to get our children to do what we believe is right. We can keep doing so until we have destroyed our relationships with them without necessarily succeeding in getting them to where we want them to be.

Remember that the core of choice theory is we choose all we do. And we begin making these choices at birth and continue to make them all our lives. Our best chance for good relationships for our whole lives is with our families. Our families would be much stronger than they are now if we could get rid of the urge to control. In *Peaceful Parenting*, Nancy teaches parents how to overcome their natural urge to control in an attempt to keep their child safe and to replace this with a loving and nurturing relationship. Whether we like it or not, parents have no control over what our children choose to do when they are on their own. Drugs, sex, alcohol and crime are all available. The only thing that may keep them from these destructive behaviors is their relationship with their parent. Learning and using choice theory as the basis for parenting is much more effective when it is used to prevent problems than to solve them. That you and your child are not adversaries makes it possible for you to give him or her some advice and likely that he or she will listen.

At present most parents and children do not realize or accept that what they are doing is chosen. Until both the child and the parent begin to learn this, they will not take responsibility for their behavior and, if it doesn't work, will blame it on someone or something else. Read this book carefully and you will see clearly how what Nancy does teaches both the child and adult to take responsibility for what they do. When they learn they are responsible, they begin to choose more effective behaviors. As they do, the role of the parent becomes more pleasant and effective. And in the process much more peaceful.

Journal of the American Medical Association (JAMA), September 10, 1997, "Protecting Adolescents from Harm." Dr. Phillip Strain, University of Colorado, Denver, Educational Psychology

William Glasser, M.D., President of The William Glasser Institute and author of *Choice Theory,* 1998, *The Language of Choice Theory,* 1999, and *Reality Therapy in Action,* 2000. All of Dr. Glasser's books are by HarperCollins.

Preface
Who am I
to Speak?

When I was growing up, I used to play with my dolls. I practiced parenting by teaching, loving and disciplining (by spanking and scolding) each doll. I was dress rehearsing skills that I would test over and over again in the actual job of parenting. I have been involved in the production of living and loving my twin sons through their babyhood, childhood and now into adolescence, as we reach the final stretch of young adulthood. Of course, one of the things that I have discovered along the way, as I maintain a relationship with my own parents and parents-in-law, is that the job of parenting never stops. But the relationship certainly changes. So does the amount of influence and responsibility. Each phase of the child's development, our own development, as well as the lives of our parents, brings new challenges and new rewards.

I am not declaring myself a success with respect to children, living in a household where never an angry word is spoken or a voice raised. This would certainly not be an honest portrayal of my life these past years. However, I can honestly say that with the help and advice of many people, including my two very wise, bright and articulate sons, our household has, for the most part, been a peaceful, loving place where together we have developed meaningful relationships with each other. We have been able to create relationships where we have been able to speak our opinions and been listened to. On frequent occasions our suggestions have been followed and implemented. Our home has been a place where we all have choices and have been able to have a say in making the rules, understanding the rules and changing the rules, as well as understanding what happens when we break the rules. We have created a place where we laugh and learn together. Each of us could probably live independently and separate from each other now (although financially both my husband and I could do this more easily and prosperously than either of the boys, at least in this stage of their lives). But we each independently choose to be with each other. The quality of our lives is improved beyond measure in our being together.

How did we get so lucky? Was it just luck? How did we get so smart? Was it just intelligence? I believe that both luck and intelligence did play a part in the beginning. By that I mean that I think both my husband and I were extremely lucky in that we were born to parents who probably had pretty good parents themselves. This luck of the draw taught us a lot about being loved and about having a relationship where we were believed in. When we met each other and finally decided to marry (we dated for six years after meeting in college), we spent a long time deciding whether or not we wanted to have children. If yes, then we wondered when we would enter that phase of our relationship. We watched our friends, our siblings and our colleagues as they made their own decisions about becoming parents. We read a lot of the popular press of the day. Here, ideas were presented, addressing parenting as both a woman and a man's responsibility. I was attempting to live my life supporting feminism as it was espoused at the time. Some of the implications were that women who chose full time parenting over career plus parenting were only continuing to fall prey to white male oppression. There were more and more options being discussed regarding the when, how and why of making the conscious choice of becoming a parent.

In addition, I was engaged in my own internal fears and war, wondering if I had what it took to be a good parent. I wondered if my husband's voiced desire to participate fully was actually going to be translated into action. My own existential turmoil led me to wonder what kind of world I was bringing a child into. Perhaps the world was too evil, corrupt and greedy. Was I only bringing a child into misery and hurt?

As you can probably gather from the above description, the women's movement was in full swing. Some of the choices and worries I faced were considerably different from those of my oldest sister, who is only five years older than I. But society's issues, questions and answers were changing. So I had many more choices, and with them felt a greater burden of responsibilities about the choices I made. Compared to my mother and my mother-in-law, my options were incredibly great. With increased options, more people were making a conscious choice about becoming parents. A deluge of books and articles emerged, as well as full magazines and classes to help parents learn the skills of parenting. So yes, we were smart and educated with information. However, sometimes all this information felt more cumbersome than helpful.

THEORETICAL FOUNDATIONS

While attending college, studying for a degree in nursing, I read a book that subsequently determined the direction of my professional life. This book, entitled *Reality Therapy,* written by psychiatrist Dr. William Glasser, articulated what I believe to be true about human beings, our life choices and our decisions in determining our own responsibilities and happiness. Following graduation, while also working as a psychiatric nurse, I began an intense study with Dr. Glasser. I pursued a master's degree in counseling while simultaneously studying Dr. Glasser's new and different explanation of human behavior. Choice theory, as he has since named it, is based on the work of William Powers who is a physicist and engineer. Powers' book, *Behavior: The Control of Perception,* explains our brain and human behavior as a control system. Studying and working with Powers, Glasser added his own ideas and observations, ultimately developing his own theory explaining human motivation and behavior.

I am profoundly grateful to Dr. Glasser for his teaching and persistent desire to understand human beings better. Because of his work, study, books and lectures, I am able to understand myself better. I have been able to share this information with others in the world. This book is my attempt to take what I have learned, apply it to parenting, and hopefully improve our understanding and work with children.

For the past twenty years, in addition to parenting my sons, I have also been traveling around the country teaching and training folks in choice theory. I have worked with people from a wide variety of professions: educators, school parents, nurses, social workers, physicians, leaders in nonprofit and for-profit organizations, hospice workers and foster care professionals, as well as foster parents. What most of these people had in common was their interest and work with other people. Sometimes they specialized in working with children. Understanding and teaching others how and why human beings behave, based on choice theory, have been profoundly rewarding to me and those I have worked with. Along the way I also received the added benefit of improved understanding of my own children, their growth and development and my job as their parent in guiding and facilitating their growth.

This book is based on choice theory, an explanation for human behavior. It is also my synthesis of choice theory and its application to parenting. As you read this book, many of the examples will be from my own personal experiences, working with and loving my own children. There are other examples that were generously shared with me by other parents, from their own parenting experiences. Still others are from my twenty years of working with professionals from all over the country, sometimes in their capacity as parents, other times in their professional capacity.

PEACEFUL PARENTING AND CHOICE THEORY

Throughout the body of this book, I have attempted to use language familiar to most readers, with two exceptions. "Quality world" is a basic theoretical construct in choice theory. Other common words, such as ideal image, wants or desires, are used interchangeably to indicate this same concept. My attempt in using this phrase to indicate Glasser's idea is to highlight the unique and important aspect of this construct. Our quality word pictures motivate all of our behaviors, from birth until death. I use this terminology not to distance the reader, but instead to underscore the importance of this idea.

The other word consistent with choice theory but potentially odd for most readers is the use of the word "power" as a verb. From a choice theory perspective, all a person can ever do, from birth to death, is behave, and all behavior is purposeful. Glasser changes many nouns, such as depression, into verbs, when discussing and presenting choice theory. Thus, "depressing" (versus being depressed) is a verb he would use to indicate the behavioral choice that people might make in attempting to change their perception of the world. For Glasser, depression is not something that happens to individuals. Rather, "depressing" is a behavioral choice people may make to try to change the world to match more closely what they want the world to be like.

In keeping with this idea, but also not wanting to confuse the reader, I have only followed this practice when using the word power. "Powering over," "powering with" and "powering within" are three phrases that I use in keeping with choice theory ideas, most specifically in Chapter 2, where I explain the "internal instructions." Again, my intent is to give the reader the flavor of the choice theory concepts without trying to beat the reader over the head with such concepts. Certainly there are many additional behaviors associated with powering over: bullying, demanding, commanding, threatening, punishing, to name a few more familiar sounding verbs that would be behaviors consistent with one person's powering over another. However, I have chosen a shorthand phrase that might include all of these behaviors. None of these behaviors might be used when one person is attempting to power over another. But the intention behind powering over would be for one person to get his own way, to control another person, through attempts to power over another.

This book is based on the existing knowledge and literature of choice theory. My contribution is to extend the application of choice theory to parenting practices, something not presently available in the choice theory literature. However, presenting a model of developmental psychology based on choice theory is my creation alone. At present, no developmental model based on the psychology of choice theory exists. Based on my own personal and professional work and study of the existing knowledge of developmental psychology, as well as my twenty plus years of work and association with other choice theorists, I have attempted to present a developmental model based on the psychology of choice theory to the existing literature in developmental psychology. As I have stated previously, choice theory is based on Glasser's work. This developmental model using choice theory is mine alone. Any shortcomings, over-extensions or errors of omission or commission that exist in the model I present rest upon my shoulders alone.

Introduction
Born with Instructions!

"This job of parenting is the hardest job of my life. Unfortunately the darn thing didn't come with instructions! Of course, I didn't have a lot of instructions on how to make a baby, but with perseverance and desire, my wife and I were able to figure that part out. How can we be expected to 'build this child into a responsible adult' without any instructions?" **John, workshop participant, Wyoming, 1993**.

What an interesting idea. Have children appear to us with instructions. Certainly all of us who are involved with helping children of any age blossom into adults can identify with the claim that child rearing is the hardest job and most rewarding experience of our lives. The challenge is great. Unfortunately, I have yet to see child-rearing instructions included with any child. And yet, many of us have been able to grow, learn and mature into happy, healthy, contributing and responsible adults, despite our parents' handicap of no instructions!

The purpose of this book is to help parents learn how to parent in successful and peaceful ways. Together, we will learn to find and read the instructions that all people are born with. In fact, once these instructions are learned, we may find they are easier to follow than some of the holiday and birthday toys that we have attempted to assemble. The results of learning and following internal instructions mean greater harmony for all in the family.

Peaceful parenting means working with our child, following the internal instructions he is born with, to help our child learn how to become a successful person. Peaceful parenting means learning to parent following our own instructions. Guided by our own and our child's instructions, we can develop and maintain a more harmonious and cooperative relationship with one another. We will be working together, each listening to and following our own internal instructions and helping each other do the same. Peaceful parenting does not mean that all aspects of our life will be free from conflict. But when we understand these internal instructions, we will learn how to resolve these conflicts with greater satisfaction for all. We will change our relationship from a struggle against each other to learning how to work with each other so both we and our child can each follow our internal instructions in harmony.

These ideas are presented for parents: biological, step or adoptive. But they apply equally to other adults involved in a child's life, including godparents, aunts, uncles, grandparents and the equally influential teachers.

OVERVIEW

This book is not a "how to" book on parenting. Rather, I am attempting to share the general ideas of choice theory as they apply to parenting. There are times that I address specific parenting issues. But readers will probably feel that some of their specific questions are left unanswered. My hope is that in sharing a general description of how and why humans behave, parents will be able to adapt choice theory ideas in helping them to solve and answer specific problems and questions.

Chapters 1 through 4 introduce the basic concepts of the human brain from a choice theory perspective. These chapters are the foundation for all the subsequent chapters. Chapter 5, "Creating a Peaceful Place for Exploration and Discovery," highlights a general "how to" application of these basic concepts. It is the heart of choice theory application in the home. Chapters 6 and 7 describe human psychological development, using choice theory as the foundation.

Chapter 8 describes, at length, "Peaceful Disciplining." For many parents, discipline is a crucial and sometimes baffling issue. Although you may feel an urge to turn immediately to this chapter if you are caught in a difficult problem with your child, I would strongly recommend that you read the preceding chapters first. "Peaceful Disciplining" is based on the foundation of understanding the human brain as described in choice theory. So reading this chapter out of sequence may lead to frustration, confusion and disappointment. If you try to apply these ideas immediately to your own personal situation, without first understanding the foundation, your chances of success will be greatly diminished. Teaching our children self-discipline is only one of the many things we do as parents. If that is all we do, whether following my ideas or not, we are probably doomed to fail. So again, I urge you to read all that precedes this chapter to understand it better, as well as increase your chances of successfully following these ideas with your own child.

Chapters 9 and 10 expand on an idea introduced earlier, that all behavior is purposeful. These chapters address more specific failure traps that parents sometimes fall into when attempting to live and work with their child. The last chapter contains final thoughts regarding the art of parenting, as well as highlighting adult responsibility to all children.

Children and parents come in both genders. However, for purposes of ease of reading I have chosen to use personal pronouns of alternating genders in alternating chapters. In all odd numbered chapters, all personal pronouns describe female children and male adults. In even numbered chapters, all personal pronouns desribe male children and female adults.

WISHES

It is my sincere hope that there will be more than one edition of this book and that subsequent editions will include specific answers to specific questions and concerns from parents who are attempting to follow these ideas as they parent.

What I hope you will find in this book is information that you can easily understand and make sense of. If you do not find this information immediately useful and contributing to the improved quality of your lives and the lives of those you live with, parent with, return the book for a full refund and write me a letter informing me of the error of my ways as well. However, I do not believe that this will be so. Because you are interested in improving and honing your parenting skills, you are reading this book. Through your reading and trying these ideas out, you can learn to parent in ways that are meaningful, loving and working towards peaceful. Along the way you may improve the quality of your life, as well as the lives of those you influence. Please write to me telling me of your successes, as well as asking questions specific to your situation. Perhaps your information will help me in writing the next edition of this book.

The internal instructions your child was born with have been written in a language that you can't immediately read. I hope this book will help you to translate those instructions. Along the way you might discover some of your own instructions, the ones you were born with, but that your parents couldn't translate, or left for you to discover on your own.

Chapter One
Decoding the Instructions

EARNING YOUR WAY OUT OF A JOB

The goal of parenting is to help our children learn how to live healthy, responsible, satisfying and fulfilling lives without us. If we do our job well, we will ultimately earn our way out of the parenting job. Of course, most parents hope that their children will remain involved with them, occasionally asking for comfort, support and advice, even when their children are able to live on their own. But the first eighteen or twenty years of a parent's job are to work toward the goal of helping his children learn to live without him.

Mother Nature is wise. She endowed each person with internal instructions to increase the chances that we will live long enough to procreate more humans, to keep this wonderful species on her planet. A parent can follow the wisdom of Mother Nature by helping his child learn to follow the internal instructions that the child is born with. If a parent does this, the goal of parenting is more easily, peacefully and successfully accomplished.

A parent can accomplish the goal of assisting his child to live independent of him without following the child's internal instructions. But this is much more difficult and potentially conflict ridden. Peace comes when a parent learns the instructions the child is born with. When a parent understands the internal instructions all humans are born with, then he can help the child learn to follow these instructions as well.

INTERNALLY MOTIVATED

The instructions that we are all born with are our internal motivation to behave. We are motivated to do things that will lead to feelings of pleasure, comfort and satisfaction. Pain, discomfort and dissatisfaction inform us when we are not following our internal instructions. Our instructions urge us to behave, to change the pain into feelings of pleasure. We know we are successfully following our internal instructions when we naturally feel good.

So, motivation for all behavior, from birth until death, comes from inside of us. Even though it may appear as if we do things because of what is happening in the world, it is our internal instruction that drives us to behave. The outside world gives us information that something in the world will aid us in following our instructions, leading to our feelings of pleasure and satisfaction. But we don't act on the things outside of us unless our internal instructions drive us to do so.

This idea can be confusing to a parent. Much of our care for our infant child involves doing things to and for our child. This can give the appearance that it is the world outside of our baby's skin that leads to her satisfaction and pleasure. But it is because our baby experiences the internal pain of hunger, that she cries, telling us it is time to feed her with bottle or breast. When the baby experiences the internal feeling of comfort and satisfaction, she knows she is following her internal instruction. The baby will no longer be internally driven to behave in ways that will lead to being fed. It is the internal motivation to behave or stop behaving that informs her of how successfully she is following her internal instructions.

As parents, we can use external motivators to help our children learn. When we externally reward our child for behaving in ways that we want, we are hoping that her feelings of pleasure that come with this reward will inspire her to repeat the behavior that we want. Or we may attempt the opposite motivator, punishing our child, hoping she will not repeat the behavior in order to avoid the pain. But when we externally reward or punish our child, we are teaching her that feelings of pleasure or pain come from outside of her. This kind of parenting will work, for a time. But ultimately, we will not have taught our child how to live her life as nature intended.

INTERNAL INSTRUCTIONS

In order for us to help our child learn successfully how to follow her internal instructions, we need to understand them ourselves. The instructions that all humans are born with are genetic. In other words, these instructions are biologically encoded. Some are physiological and structural, aiding in our physical survival. One genetic instruction, for example, drives us to stand erect, walking on our hind legs. Without assistance, all children reach an age where they begin attempting to follow this genetic instruction. A parent works with the child, guiding and supporting her, as she attempts to follow this instruction. But the child receives the urge to stand and walk as part of her encoded genetic instructions.

Our social and psychological genetic instructions drive our behavior, as well. It is the psychological genetic instructions that we will be addressing in this book. Following these instructions not only enables our physical survival, but also facilitates living our life with others.

All of our instructions, whether physical or psychological, are genetically encoded to enable humans to survive, living long enough to reach the age of sexual maturity. At sexual maturity, humans are then able to procreate, producing more humans. This process is Mother Nature's way of ensuring that the species of humans will continue.

THE BIOLOGICAL NEED — SURVIVAL

Survival is the first instruction we will discuss. This instruction carries with it a drive to behave, biologically as well as psychologically, in ways that will increase the chances of surviving. The biological aspects of survival include the drive to eat when we are hungry, drink when we are thirsty, seek warm and protected shelter, breathe fresh air and eliminate waste products from our bodies, as well as engage in sexual relations once we reach the age of sexual maturity. No one has to teach us these instructions, although initially others, usually our parents, provide many of these necessities for us. Each of us is born, driven to procure those things necessary for our very survival.

We all reach an age where we can consciously ignore these urges. Thus, by choice, people are able to eat very restricted diets, hold their breath for long periods of time, spend long periods of time outdoors in perilous temperatures, as well as choose to live a celibate life. But to ignore our biological instructions to survive, we make a conscious decision to feel our internal urge and not act on it. By nature, we are born driven to behave to satisfy our biological need to survive.

In addition to the instructions to behave to insure our biological survival, we are also born with other genetic instructions, all ensuring our healthy survival. Although not as imminently perilous if ignored for a time, the psychological instructions are equally important. The psychological genetic instructions drive us to behave, to meet these instructions. When followed, we not only survive,but are able to lead happy and fulfilled lives. Mother Nature was not only concerned about our survival, but she was also concerned about the quality of our life.

We all reach an age where we can consciously choose to ignore our internal signal to survive biologically. We can choose to behave in ways that will lead to our destruction and death, suicide being the most obvious example. But our psychological instructions enable us to experience happiness and pleasure, enjoying the quality of our continued survival.

The psychological genetic instructions are the need for safety and security (the psychological aspect of survival), the need to love and belong, the need to be powerful, the need to have fun and the need to be free. We will discuss each of these need instructions in some depth. But know that each of these needs developed as part of our genetic instructions to increase our chances of surviving. We are driven to behave in ways that will continue our survival. All of these instructions aid in our individual survival, as well as the survival of the species.

THE PSYCHOLOGICAL NEEDS
THE NEED FOR SAFETY
AND SECURITY

When our ancestors lived a more primitive life, the need to feel safe and secure increased the chances of individuals' surviving. Staying among the group, a person could feel some assurance that this security would keep him from harm. Staying in the warm and protected shelter, a person felt safer from the potentially dangerous elements and predators. Young ones felt safe and secure in their mothers' arms or fathers' laps. Feeling safe and secure meant the child could venture off to explore regions that were still a safe distance from the protection of parent and family, but might lead to a discovery that would assist the whole group's survival.

Although we do not live in the primitive conditions of our ancestors, the instruction to feel safe and secure still keeps young ones from straying too far from the immediate protection of an adult. Feeling safe in our own abilities to cope with the unexpected, allows us to explore and expand our knowledge of our world and our abilities. Curiosity, another instruction we will discuss shortly, drives us to explore the world. But the instruction to feel secure keeps us from exploring too far beyond our safety zone.

When, lodging in a hotel, many people will secure every lock on their door, as well as review the instructions posted on the back of the door that explain safe exiting in case of fire. Completing these tasks is following their instruction to feel safe and secure. Other folks will call home, informing family members of the telephone number where they can be reached in case of an emergency. Again, following the instruction for safety, they are sharing the information with their family to help them feel safe and secure. All of these behaviors are driven by genetic instruction to feel safe and secure.

Sometimes we find ourselves in situations where we "get in over our head." Feeling we could handle what was before us, we proceeded, only to find ourselves in a place where we did not feel safe or secure. Traveling home late at night on a deserted country road, we realize that we have a flat tire. Some people may experience a queasy feeling in their gut, realizing they are not feeling safe in this situation. Television advertisements encourage us to purchase cellular phones or pagers, telling us that owning such devices will aid in our feelings of safety and security.

Young children calling out to their parent at night, beckoning their parent to chase away the bogeyman in the closet, are feeling driven by their need for safety and security. Horror stories that pre-adolescents and adolescents tell one another about the perils of entering middle school or high school, are all following the need to feel safe and secure.

When we follow our genetic instruction to feel safe and secure, we are able to move out of the safety zone and explore more of the world and our abilities in the world. If we do not feel safe, however, we will not go far afield.

THE NEED FOR LOVE
AND BELONGING

When our ancestors, living in caves, were trying to survive the dangers threatening much of their daily life, they discovered that there was safety in numbers. This discovery led to their internal instruction to belong, to be part of a group. We are social creatures, craving and seeking other humans for company and companionship. Part of this drive includes the sexual urge to find someone to mate with, guaranteeing the survival of the species. But the drive to love and be loved, to belong and feel connected to a group, is more than a sexual urge.

When we enter a large group, perhaps a meeting or a church social, the first thing we do is to look around the room, to see who is there that we can feel connected to. We greet friends and enjoy the returned greeting. If we attend a meeting where we know no one, we will quickly seek an introduction, someone with whom we can feel connected. We are following our genetic instruction to belong.

In addition, we will seek more intimate, connected relationships in our lives. These are the people that we love and feel love us. This special sense of belonging, that we call love, may include a sexual relationship, but not always. The love I share with my sisters, for example, is not a sexual relationship. A child learns that the loving relationship she shares with her parent satisfies her need for love and belonging. Then the sense of love and belonging extends beyond the parent-child relationship to include all in the extended family. A child feels she belongs to her class at school, to her neighborhood, to various clubs and activities. All of these relationships help the

child to satisfy her internal instruction to belong, to feel connected, to give and receive love.

When a person does not follow this instruction, he feels sad,
lonely and isolated. These feelings are urging him to behave,
get connected, give and receive love. A baby may begin to cry
when left alone in a playpen or crib. Dad, hearing the cry, goes
in to check on the baby. When he arrives, baby sees him and
immediately stops crying and begins smiling. She was feeling
lonely, the pain of not meeting her need to belong. When Dad
appeared, the baby once again felt connected and was able to
satisfy her need for love and belonging.

Television advertisements beckon us to purchase some
product, guaranteeing our sense of belonging, being connected
to a group, if we purchase the item. "Be a part of the Pepsi
generation" or "Generation Next," the ad tells us. If we buy
what they are selling, we will belong, be part of the group.

The genetic instruction for love and belonging urges us to
behave in ways that help us to develop and sustain relationships
with others in our life. This need drives us to develop connections with others, leading to a sense of belonging, being part
of a group, and ultimately to giving and receive love.

THE NEED FOR POWER

Not only are we driven to be part of a group, connected to
other human beings, we are also driven to stand out as unique
and special individuals. Each person seeks personal recognition for some contribution he can make to the group,
improving the group because he is part of it.

It may be easy to recognize how this genetic instruction
helped our ancestors to survive. The most powerful in the
group got the best slice of meat or the prized sleeping location
closest to the fire. The most powerful group of people could
beat the weaker group in the hunt.

Today there are examples from bullies in the playground to
world governments bullying neighboring nations, all attempting
to gain power. In our society, money equals power. Those with
the most money are seen as those who wield the most power
and influence to "get their own way." These are examples of
people powering OVER other people in order to follow the

instruction to be powerful. Although our instructions do not include how to behave in ways that allow us to meet our needs without interfering with other people's ability to meet their needs, there is an advantage when we learn this. (This is something we will discuss in greater depth in Chapter 8, "Peaceful Disciplining.") In other words, we learn that we are better able to meet our need for power   when we learn to power with other people as well as meet our need for power within ourselves. When we follow our instruction for power this way, it allows us to stay involved with other people, so we are better able to follow all of our genetic instructions.

Our ancestors discovered this as well. When someone in the group developed and honed a skill that others in the group were not able to accomplish but that helped the group as a whole, he received recognition and status. If he became the medicine man, or the tool maker, or the most skilled and artistic weaver, or the keenest hunter, or the most skilled explorer, each of these skills not only benefitted the individual, but the whole group. Often these experts became the teachers that others apprenticed under, learning the skill and ability, and carrying it to the next generation so the group could continue to benefit. Thus, people learned that following the instruction to be powerful within themselves (e.g., developing a skill or craft), as well as powerful with others in the group, would enhance the survival of the group. Even though it may be easy to recognize that powering over others is a person's urge to follow genetic instructions, so is powering with and powering within.

Children who learn to hold their bottles, placing them in their mouths when they want and taking them out when they want, are following their genetic instruction for power. When my son learned to zip his jacket by himself, I could see the sparkle in his eye. He could now reach his coat, put it on and zip it up all by himself. He had learned a series of effective behaviors to help him meet his need for power. He did not have power over me but certainly was able to meet his internal instruction for power within himself.

When we give our children information of any sort, we are aiding in their ability to meet their need for power. Knowing ahead of time that the family has evening plans to visit family members helps a child develop her own plans. So when information is shared about various activities and schedules, all increase their opportunity to follow their instruction for power.

Television advertisements are full of products, that if purchased, guarantee our successful ability to follow our genetic instruction for power. Laundry detergents promise to whiten and brighten clothes more than neighbors' clothes. Various sneakers promise to help us jump higher, run faster, win whatever sport played. If we purchase the right kind of automobile, we are also guaranteed greater social status, a speedier ride or the luxury we deserve. Once again, Madison Avenue advertising executives demonstrate that they are knowledgeable of the genetic instructions people are born with. They promise happiness and fulfillment in following our needs by simply purchasing whatever they are selling.

When we successfully follow our instruction to be powerful, we are seeking recognition. We want to impact and contribute to the group, making a positive difference. This genetic instruction drives us to behave in ways that will help us experiment and achieve. In an attempt to gain recognition, we behave in unique ways, potentially benefitting not only ourselves, but the group.

THE NEED FOR FUN

The genetic instruction for fun drives us to play and explore the world. The satisfaction that came when this need was met kept our ancestors curious, continuing to explore and learn. Our species has much to learn in order to be able to live independent of parents. Having a genetic instruction that drives us to explore, giving us good, pleasurable feelings, helps us to continue to be curious and to learn. When we learn something new, we experience a good feeling inside. Playing, learning, discovering and seeking to understand are the behaviors that help us satisfy this need for fun.

Children follow this instruction without hesitation. They certainly do not wait until they reach school to begin learning. They are learning all the time. Watch a baby who discovers that a smaller cup fits inside a larger cup. She will continue to place smaller inside larger, over and over again, with squeals of delight. She has learned something, and it feels wonderful! All children follow this genetic instruction to play, learn and explore.

Unfortunately, when some people reach adulthood, they fail to continue to recognize this genetic instruction. But play, curiosity and discovery are important drives, no matter what age. Adults who continue to follow this instruction also experience the pleasure and delight that come from learning something new.

Understanding this instruction can aid in the job of parenting. Instead of trying to curtail our child from having fun, we can use our child's instruction to be playful and have fun. Turning serious work or a boring task into a game, help both parent and child successfully and more willingly do the work.

🏠 🏠 🏠 🏠

Another evening, returning home well past the boys' bedtime, I want the boys in bed, but I want them to perform all of their get-ready-for-bed rituals first. How can I convince the boys to behave efficiently, so they can hurry to bed for a good night's sleep?

Other times when I've been faced with this challenge, I nag or whine, hoping to hurry them along. This never works. In fact, the whole routine seems to take longer.

Tonight I am inspired. As we enter the house, I challenge the boys. "I bet I can get changed into my night clothes, with my teeth brushed, before either of you can."

That's all it takes. The game is on. We race up the stairs, quickly changing into our pajamas and brushing our teeth. I do not try to let the boys win, but they do. Of course, as an adult, I need to hang up some clothes and fold others neatly. These details don't matter to the boys.

🏠 🏠 🏠 🏠

The times I remember to change a chore or a task into something fun, like a game we can all play, I am much more successful in getting cooperation from my sons. This helps not only my children, but also me. We are born driven to play, laugh and learn. We are curious, wanting to know and understand our world and our place in it, as well as our own abilities.

Too often we adults spend time admonishing a child to "stop having fun," or telling them "we have serious work to do." Unfortunately, when we make such statements, we are asking a child to go against her very nature. Instead, we can learn better how to follow our own genetic instruction to play and have fun by watching a child as our example.

Our genetic instruction for fun is our genetic pay-off for learning. Children have much to learn in order to be able to live on their own. The genetic instruction for fun facilitates this learning.

THE NEED FOR FREEDOM

The genetic instruction for freedom generates our desire for choices and options in our life. As a culture, we have a great deal of freedom. In fact, our country is founded on the basic right of freedom for all. The biological advantage for freedom enabled our ancestors to survive. If a group experienced a drought or some other natural phenomenon that prevented people from eating their usual diet, other choices for nutrition could be made. Not all animals are so lucky. Panda bears, for example, eat the new leaves of a specific kind of bamboo plant. When these bamboo plants are in short supply, the very existence of the Panda bears as a species is at risk. Humans can (and many do) eat a wide variety of foods for sustenance and life.

Not only do we want freedom and choices in our diet, but in all other aspects of following our other genetic instructions as well. We each want to know that we have enough options to be able to feel safe, be loved, feel powerful, and have fun. The drive for freedom or choices ensures that we will have what we need for our physical as well as psychological survival.

When we are not able to meet our need for freedom we feel restricted. However, Victor Frankl, who was imprisoned in a Nazi concentration camp, speaks of the freedom within our mind and emotions, even when we are imprisoned, seemingly without choices or options. The history of humankind is replete with examples of people fighting to their death, attempting to gain their basic freedom.

Part of the art of parenting is providing our children with the freedom they need in order to meet their other basic needs, but to do this in a way that keeps our child safe. If we provide our child with more freedom than she has responsible behaviors to handle, she may be or feel unsafe. If we do not provide enough freedom for our child when she has the responsible behaviors to handle additional freedom, she will feel restricted, unable to meet her other basic needs. A parent needs to balance providing additional freedom for the child while simultaneously teaching her new, responsible behaviors to cope with the additional freedom. This is the art of teaching the child self-discipline. We will address this issue at length in Chapter 8, "Peaceful Disciplining".

An added benefit to helping our child learn effective behaviors to follow her genetic instruction for freedom is that we then become better able to meet our need for freedom. Teaching your child to choose her own clothes, choose whether water or juice will quench her thirst, choose the bedtime story to be read, choose her own time to complete homework assignments, choose what classes to take in high school, frees the parent from having to make all of these decisions and choices for the child. The more choices we give to our child, assisting her to determine how to make good choices, the more we are free from having to do things for our child. We move in the direction of doing things WITH our child, the position we want to be in when our child is able to live independently.

SAME NEEDS —DIFFERENT PICTURES

The basic psychological needs or genetic instructions are the same for all human beings. We are all born, driven to satisfy our need for safety and security, our need for love and belonging, our need for power, our need for fun and our need for freedom. Although we all share these needs, not every person has the same ideas of what will be need-satisfying. Through our different experiences in the world, we feel the pleasure and comfort that accompany need satisfaction. Each person has unique experiences and subsequently different ideas of what will be need-satisfying. (This idea is discussed at length in Chapter 2, "Quality -What Do You Want?")

Although I have described examples of need satisfaction, the description is not complete. That is because not every person has the same definition of following his genetic instruction for fun, for example, in the same way. Tennis is a game that I play frequently, enjoying the pleasure and challenge of keeping the tennis ball in the court and away from my opponent. This game is a satisfying picture of how I meet my need for fun, power, freedom and love and belonging. Certainly not everyone reading this book would agree with this idea, however. Although we all share the same genetic instructions, we do not all share the same idea of what is need-satisfying.

EFFECTIVE BEHAVIORS

We are born with the genetic instructions driving us to satisfy our needs in the world. Although television commercials try to entice us to purchase their products as ways to follow our genetic instructions successfully, this is not what nature intended. Purchasing something is not an effective way to satisfy our genetic instructions. It is through our behavior that we discover that we are able to follow our instructions effectively. We are driven to behave in the world to satisfy our genetic instructions. We meet our needs through our relationships with self, other people and our activities, as well as through places, things and beliefs. A parent's job is to help his child learn effective behaviors leading to the child's feeling the pleasure and comfort that come with meeting a basic need, successfully following her genetic instructions. If parents first understand what their child's instructions are, then help the child learn a wide range of effective behaviors that will help the child meet her needs, the parents have accomplished the parenting job successfully. Peaceful parenting means understanding and following our own genetic instructions as well as helping our child listen and follow her genetic instructions.

MEET NEEDS DAILY

Our genetic instructions drive us to behave in the world to ensure our survival, including the quality of our survival. These genetic instructions drive us to behave moment to moment, hourly and daily, in the same way we are driven to eat and sleep regularly, so we will continue to survive. Our other genetic instructions drive us to behave regularly, so we meet our needs daily. We can live our lives without meeting one or more of our psychological needs daily, but the quality of our lives suffer. Similarly, we can deprive ourselves of food for days at a time, but this deprivation creates uncomfortable, unpleasant internal feelings.

Not only are we driven to meet all of our psychological needs daily, following all of our instructions leads to more balance and satisfaction. In other words, we cannot get enough love to satisfy our need for power. The instructions for both love and power must be followed. In Chapter 5, "Creating a Peaceful Place," we will discuss this idea further, but the job of a parent is to create opportunities within the home for all people to meet all of their needs on a daily basis. When a child learns how to meet her need for safety, love, power, fun and freedom at home, she will have a greater ability to meet her same needs away from home. Other places may not provide as many positive opportunities for the child to meet her needs, but if she learns a wide range of effective behaviors at home, she will be better able to handle those situations where fewer opportunities exist.

TEMPORARY POWER DIFFERENTIAL

As we have already discussed, one way people can follow their instruction to be powerful is to have power over others. Powering over another means meeting the need for power by interfering with another person's ability to meet his needs. Although this will work, the inevitable consequence of such a choice is that the person we power over, will ultimately move away from us, attempting to be disconnected and separated from us.

At birth, however, a power differential naturally exists between us and our child. Obviously, when our child is small, we have the ability to remove our child physically from situations where we do not want her, for example. The ability to think and speak are more effective for a parent than for a child. Because we are physically and mentally stronger than our child, we have the possibility to power over our child, to exert our will more successfully to get our way.

Initially, when our child is small, powering over our child so we "win" (and the child loses) may result in our child's pouting or crying in her attempt to meet her needs successfully. These behaviors can be easily ignored by a parent. But eventually the child will grow, so she is no longer physically and mentally inferior to the parent. Eventually a parent who attempts to impose his will on his child through physical, mental or emotional force, may meet with equally strong physical, mental or emotional resistance. The child may decide to move away from the parent, disconnecting and separating, either physically, mentally or emotionally. This is something parents want to avoid.

When a parent recognizes that from birth a natural power differential exists between himself and his child, the parent can begin to help both himself and his child learn to meet their needs effectively for power without powering over each other. That means both parent and child should concentrate on learning effective behaviors to meet their need for power by learning power within (personal internal recognition) and power with each other. Even though a parent can follow his genetic instruction for power by powering over his child, he needs to work continually to help his child learn how to follow her genetic instructions without powering over the child. The power differential that naturally exists at birth is something a parent should work to change, moving to an eventual parity of power between parent and child.

KEEPING LOVE ALIVE

As was already discussed, we are all born with the genetic instruction to develop loving relationships. This instruction drives both parent and child to develop a loving relationship with each other. For our child, her loving relationship with us is the first loving relationship she experiences in the world. This initial relationship of the love between parent and child formulates for our child her first impression of what a loving relationship is like, with the accompanying pleasurable and comforting feelings for need fulfillment. It will influence all subsequent loving relationships in our child's life.

In order for a parent to influence and teach the child effective behaviors to help her follow her genetic instructions, the parent must maintain a loving relationship with the child. Because our child believes we love her, have her best interests at heart, and will avoid hurting her, she will more likely listen and be influenced by us and by our wise words of counsel as well as imitating our behaviors.

The most important and vital aspect of the parent-child relationship then is maintaining a loving, connected relationship with one another. It takes a great deal of painful, negative interactions between parent and child before the child will choose to disconnect from her parent. Unfortunately, all of us may be acutely aware of abusive and unloving relationships that exist between some parents and children. Even then, some may wish that the child would separate and move away from such destructive parents, yet the child continues to stay involved and connected. Biologically, this makes sense. Children are born intuitively knowing that their very life and survival depend on maintaining their relationship with the primary care-giver, the parent.

It is imperative then that a parent follow the genetic instruction to be loving and connected with his child. It takes a lot for a child to want to move away from the love she feels for her parent. The same is also true for a parent. However, to insure that parent and child will stay connected with one another, everything that occurs between parent and child should be heavily coated and covered with love. When faced with difficulties or doubt about our parenting abilities or problems our child is having, we need to let our love, our sense of belonging to one another, and our desire to stay connected to each other, be our guide in helping us determine what to do. When in doubt, love.

SUMMARY

- The goal of parenting is to teach our child all she needs to know to be able to live independent of her parents.
- All humans are born with internal instructions to ensure the survival of the individual. In addition, these instructions

increase the chances that the species of humans will also survive.

• Peaceful parenting occurs when a parent learns the internal instructions the child is born with and helps the child learn these instructions.

• Peaceful parenting means understanding and following our own genetic instructions as well as helping our child listen and follow her genetic instructions.

• Internal feelings of pleasure, comfort and satisfaction come when we follow our instructions. Pain, discomfort and dissatisfaction come when we are not successfully following our instructions.

• Pain motivates us to behave, to do something, to change the pain into feelings of pleasure, so we more successfully follow our genetic instructions.

• A parent can use external rewards or punishment to attempt to teach or change the child's behavior, but this is going against the child's nature, her internal genetic instructions.

• Our genetic instructions are encoded into our biology. Some exist for our physical survival. Our psychological genetic instructions help to improve the quality of our life, so we will want to continue to live.

• Our psychological genetic instructions are the need for safety and security, the need of love and belonging, the need for power, the need for fun, the need for freedom. Each of these needs arises from and contributes to the need for physical survival.

• Although all humans are born with the same genetic instructions, we all have a wide variety of people, places, activities, things, behaviors and beliefs that will satisfy our needs.

• Our genetic instructions drive us to behave to meet our needs. We must learn effective behaviors to satisfy our needs. A parent's job is to help the child learn effective behaviors.

• Just as we need to eat and sleep daily, we must follow our genetic instructions and meet our needs daily. A parent's job is to create a home environment where all members can meet their needs daily.

● A natural power differential exists between parent and child. A parent's job is to help the child learn effective behaviors without powering over the child, to help her learn. The parent's goal is to work toward power parity between parent and child.

● A parent should work to maintain a loving relationship with his child. This not only helps the child formulate her ideas about subsequent loving relationships, it also enables the parent to continue to influence the child's learning. When in doubt, love.

Chapter Two
Quality World –
What Do We Want?

BUILDING DREAMS

As we live our lives in the world, we are driven to follow our genetic instructions. We develop specific ideas of what we want that we believe will best follow these instructions. Each of us has a specific picture of what would be playful and meet our need for fun, for example. The places and activities which we could enjoy where playful behaviors are successful in helping us meet our need for fun are individual and specifically unique to each of us.

Our ideas, dreams and aspirations are the pictures in our quality world (what we want) that we imagine will allow us to follow our genetic instructions successfully and meet our needs. The quality world is the part of our consciousness that holds all that is of importance, high value and meaning to us. We believe or have experiences of meeting our basic genetic needs through these quality world pictures and ideas.

As parents read this book, some may be aware of their own basic needs, their own genetic instructions that we have talked about thus far. Others may be less aware of these needs and instructions but may be more aware of what they want. Most have some kind of an idea or picture in their heads of what they hope to learn from this book. The idea exists in their heads that by reading this book they will learn parenting skills that are more peaceful. This idea is what inspired them to read the book to begin with.

There are other wants and desires we may be aware of: the kind of weather we hope tomorrow will bring as we plan a family picnic, the outcome of a conversation we will have with our boss the next time our annual review is due, the best dessert we can imagine eating, the place we would love to vacation if money were no obstacle in preventing us from doing whatever we want. All of these ideas are total sensory moving pictures of what we want in our lives that we believe will help us satisfy our needs and successfully follow our genetic instructions. These pictures make up what we will call the "quality world."

Throughout all of our lives, each of us has been building our quality world pictures of all the people, places, activities and things that we believe will meet our basic needs. The pictures are moving pictures with not only people, places and things built into the scene but also included are the behaviors we use to satisfy our needs and follow our genetic instructions. Each of us is the star in these unique moving pictures. We put the pictures into our quality world when our real world experiences result in the very good feeling of our needs being met.

For instance, the first time some of us ate ice cream we experienced a strong good feeling at the same time our hungry feelings were satisfied. So ice cream became a picture in our quality world. For me, coffee ice cream is a strong picture in my quality world because it was the most fun activity I engaged in as a young child during boring, obligatory visits to distant and elderly family relatives. The highlight of the day was when my great aunt offered us ice cream. The only flavor she had in the house was coffee. At the time this was not my favorite, but any flavor ice cream was better than none. Many years later coffee ice cream has become my favorite flavor. I associate this delicious treat not only with satisfying my survival need of hunger, but also with fun reminders of family time, satisfying the need for love and belonging.

We may also have a vague notion that our needs will be met through an experience that we haven't actually had but have learned or heard about from someone else. So this idea of what we may want becomes a hoped for need-fulfilling picture in our quality world. For instance, when we were deciding on a career or job for ourselves, we may not have had actual experience with the job, but the limited information that we had led us to believe that this job would suit us. After we actually began working in the job, we may have been lucky enough to realize that all we hoped for in this job was a reality, and much more satisfaction, pleasure and fun could be derived from this job. These additions were things that we didn't even realize were part of the job. But all these aspects of the job helped us meet our needs for power, fun and belonging. So our chosen profession became a strong picture in our quality world.

This same experience may have occurred for us when we became a parent. We may have had a vague idea of all the pleasures and potential difficulties of parenting. But once this idea became a reality, our experience has probably been fuller, richer and much more satisfying than we ever dreamed it would be. The notion of being a parent was a hoped for picture in our quality world before the children came along. Now that they are here, parenting is still very much a part of our quality world, only it is a clearer, fuller and more satisfying picture.

Before we begin spinning off into a guilty reverie because we don't always feel loving or positive toward our children, let me explain that I am only talking about the ideal pictures of what being a parent is all about. In our quality world we hold the pictures of all the positive, need-fulfilling experiences. Our quality world pictures are like never ending commercials of the ideal, thus the name quality indicating only the best, the supreme, the ultimate. There are certainly moments in our lives with our children where the ugly, messy and less than idyllic occur. This is in the real world, a notion we will address further on in this chapter as well as the next. For now we are only discussing those quality world pictures where life is sweet and satisfying, where we are able to follow our genetic instructions successfully and meet our basic needs.

The pictures in our quality world are not all of equal value. The experience of something that *is* need-fulfilling is of higher value than an idea that something *will be* need-fulfilling in the future. Those pictures that meet more than one need are of higher value than those that meet only one need. So the picture I have of family vacations is of higher value than the picture I have of my car, for example. With my car I meet my needs for safety, survival and freedom. On a family vacation I meet all of my needs.

WHAT MOTIVATES BEHAVIOR?

These pictures in our quality world, essentially our desires, are what motivates all behavior. I am born with the instruction to love, a basic need. But I am motivated to maintain a loving relationship with my husband because he is the person in my quality world with whom I get satisfaction for following this basic instruction. In other words, the needs or instructions are generic or general. The quality world pictures are the specific pictorial representation of what is need-fulfilling. It is the desire to have these quality world pictures become a reality that motivates all of our behaviors from birth until death. Parents are motivated to read this book because of the hoped for picture in their quality world of learning peaceful parenting. They will stop reading this book and proceed with their next task motivated by another picture in their quality world, perhaps eating a satisfying meal or preparing to go out with a friend for the evening, or doing the laundry. The ideal of need satisfaction represented in a quality world picture motivates us to behave in the real world so that our ideals become reality in our life.

We have many pictures in our quality world. As we have already discussed, we have five basic needs. Each of the needs has many pictures in our quality world that are satisfying. So my need for love and belonging has pictures of not only my husband, but of my family, friends and some colleagues. I do not meet my need for love and belonging with everyone that I meet, so not everyone I encounter in my life is in my quality world. The people that are in my quality world are not all of equal value. Some friends are more precious to me than others, and family members are closer to my heart than are my colleagues.

I behave in the world to maintain these loving relationships. I am driven to behave by my genetic instructions, and I am motivated to behave lovingly toward the specific people in my quality world with whom I meet my need for love and belonging.

CONFLICTS ARISE

Understanding this idea can be helpful when we live in a world with so many people who have such varying ideas about the way things should be in the world. Each person is describing her own quality world picture when she tells you the way the world should be. All individuals are driven to behave in a specific way in order to change the world to match their quality world ideal. "Too many cooks spoil the broth" because each chef has her own idea of what the perfect broth looks, tastes and smells like. When too many chefs try simultaneously to prepare the perfect broth, usually none of them is satisfied. Some of the guests at the dinner table may remark about the delicious, unique flavor of this broth. But probably all of the chefs will say the broth has been spoiled because it is not living up to each one's expectation of her broth in her quality world.

The beginning of any relationship is the discovery of what the other person's quality world consists of. This can be quite shocking, sometimes fun and funny, and can sometimes lead to anger and disagreements. How to squeeze a tube of toothpaste may be a very specific picture in our spouse's quality world. We may not even have been aware that a method for squeezing the tube exists. Our spouse may be equally shocked to discover our haphazard, care-free method with the toothpaste tube. Similar kinds of experiences may surround other household placements and tasks. What is the proper way to put toilet paper on the roll dispenser? What is the proper temperature setting for the thermostat? What is the ideal dinner time? What is the proper method for paying bills? What is the ideal budget? How much is set aside for savings? And on it goes. Some of these things may be relatively trivial and innocuous. But others, such as the family's religious practice, can be significant and of utmost importance in a relationship.

I remember how surprised I was when my husband announced we were not going to get a family dog because we already had a family cat. Each household should have only one pet, according to the picture in his quality world. When he was growing up, his family had only one pet, a dog. For him to agree to a cat was already a stretch. When I was growing up, my family had both a cat and a dog. So my quality world picture included a family with both a cat and a dog. Luckily, this was not too highly valued a picture in either of our quality worlds so we were able to be flexible about adapting and compromising our quality world pictures. In developing the relationship we were able to develop new quality world pictures that included each other. As a result, we were willing to negotiate and modify old quality world pictures.

I was also surprised when my husband and I were returning from our honeymoon and began to discuss finances. In retrospect I now realize that having this discussion prior to our marriage would have been a more ideal time. However, his idea of when to pay bills was very different from mine. Additionally, my thought was that each of us would keep our own private bank account as well as opening a joint account. My husband had no such idea. Our assumption of our financial lives was based on two very different quality world pictures.

Similarly, as parents we have pictures in our quality world of what and how a parent will behave. If parents are part of a couple who is parenting, then they probably have already faced situations where they and their partner have very different ideas of how to parent. Similarly, if the family is a blended family where there are more than two parents, the ideas of how to handle various child-rearing issues become even more complicated because each adult has a unique quality world picture of how a parent and a child should behave. We should not leave out the grandparents with their own quality world pictures and ideas of parenting. Awareness of this concept can help to alleviate some of the disagreements that may have been sore points for us and the other adults who are involved with our child. Each of us has our own opinions based on our own quality world view of the way the world should be that would be the most need satisfying for us.

As a parent we develop pictures of ourselves as parents. And we develop pictures FOR our children. Much of the disagreements and arguments that arise between parent and child are due to our differing pictures.

🏠   🏠   🏠   🏠

The calendar reads spring. The day is sunny. The temperature this morning is hovering around 50 degrees. A 12-year old child arrives at the breakfast table dressed for school in shorts. The picture in his head is that dressing for the season does not necessarily involve dressing for the temperature.

Mother: *"You're not wearing those shorts to school today. It's too cold."*

Son: "*I'm not cold. Besides, everybody has been wearing them.*"

Mother: "*I don't care about everybody. It's too cold. And besides, you'll get sick if you go to school dressed   like that.*"

Son: "*I can't believe you. You're so old fashioned.*"

🏠   🏠   🏠   🏠

The above scene is describing different pictures between mother and son. Mother has a picture of her son dressing nicely, warm and comfortable enough to concentrate on learning in school. The son is dressed hoping for the fun-filled days of spring, with increased freedom. He is also dressing to be accepted by his friends, wanting to wear what other "cool kids" are wearing. Although both mom and son have the same genetic instructions, each has a very different quality world picture. The son, driven by his strong belonging instruction as he enters adolescence, wants to dress in a way that is seen as "cool" and acceptable by his peers. He is willing to sacrifice his survival instruction of warmth and comfort in order to feel that he fits in with his peers. Mom also wants her son to be accepted by his friends, but the mom's instruction of keeping her son free from illness is a much stronger drive at this time. Each is following similar genetic instructions, but the pictures of how these instructions can be best followed are very different for each of them. Their quality world pictures are colliding. (For resolution, turn to similar situation in Table 1 on page 35.)

INFLUENCING OUR CHILD'S QUALITY WORLD

Children are not blank slates awaiting our etching of their ideal quality world pictures. From birth on, each child has experiences in the world that have been need-satisfying, following his own genetic instructions. Each of these events resulted in a quality world picture of the way he wants the world to be so that it is most satisfying to him.

Luckily, much of what occurs in our children's lives that is need-satisfying involves us. So the quality world pictures often are very similar within a family. Because we live with our children, we have great influence on many of the pictures that they put into their quality world. Our child's favorite meal is probably a meal that we prepare for him. Every member of my family is an avid and enthusiastic skier. We introduced this activity into our children's lives early because skiing was an activity that both my husband and I enjoyed. We didn't want to give up skiing, so instead we introduced it to our children. Because the activity was need-fulfilling for the boys, they added it to their quality world. However, I have not been able to influence successfully my children's taste in how they dress. Over-sized shirts and pants worn well below the waist are the style that their generation has adopted. My children have embraced this picture into their quality worlds of the appearance they want. I can offer my opinion with the hope that I might influence and change their minds. But I must be careful how often I do such a thing because eventually my opinion can begin to feel too much like criticism. Then I run the risk that my children will take me out of their quality world all together. (For more on this, see Chapter 10, "Criticism - A Destructive Habit".)

Each of us has the same genetic instructions. But our interpretation and understanding of how we will behave in the world to meet our needs are based on the pictures in our quality world. They are unique and individual.

As parents, our job is to provide opportunities for our children to meet their needs and follow their genetic instructions. We will discuss this idea in much greater depth in Chapter 5, "Creating a Peaceful Place". For now, suffice it to say that our job is to provide opportunities for our children to discover how and where they can meet their needs. As adults who have lived longer in the world, we have more experiences and thus more pictures in our quality world of need-fulfilling opportunities. Our children are continuously greeting the world as a new experience. Some previous experiences are solid pictures in their quality worlds. Others are only hoped for pictures. Much of their life involves trying out new behaviors, new experiences to see if basic needs can be satisfied. As parents, we are presented with the difficult task of learning the art of parenting. That is, allowing our children opportunities to interact and explore the world to discover what is and is not need-fulfilling but to do this in a way that keeps them safe.

This is more easily done when our children are small, under our constant watch and supervision. However, when children enter adolescence, they are not so closely monitored by us. Helping them to meet their freedom instruction means that our children are spending greater and greater periods of time away from us. This also means that we may have very specific ideas of what we want and don't want for our children based on the pictures in our quality world. But our children have ideas of what they want and don't want based on the pictures in their quality worlds.

As a parent, we may want to limit the amount of time our four-year old watches television. If we spend our days and evenings with our child, we can monitor our quality world into becoming a reality. But when our child reaches age nine, spending more time at friends' houses, we may not be there to regulate this quality world standard. We may believe that our 14-year old daughter is too young to wear makeup. Before she leaves the house every day for school, we eat breakfast with her and see that our idea about makeup is followed. But our daughter may decide to get to school early, go to the girls' room and apply her makeup for the day. At the end of the day she removes the makeup before she returns home where we will see her. She is motivated by two different pictures in her quality world. She wants to see herself as a powerful young woman who can wear makeup when she sees fit, no matter what her parents think. And she also wants to maintain her loving relationship with her parent, which means following her parent's desires and rules. So this child chooses sneaking and deceitful behaviors in order to get both the pictures that she wants from her quality world.

As distressing as this information might be to some parents, probably all can relate because we may have had similar experiences when we were adolescents. We didn't want to disobey our parents, but we wanted what we thought was best, motivated by the pictures in our own quality world that may have been in direct conflict with our parents' rules motivated by the pictures in our parents' quality worlds. Although we may not have been as bold as the above young woman, we probably had wishes to act defiantly even if we did not act upon these thoughts. We were attempting to meet our needs for power and freedom but didn't want to hurt our parents' feelings or get into trouble with them.

NEGOTIATING QUALITY WORLD

With this new understanding and highlighted dilemma that we face as parents, the question is how do we proceed? Do we simply abandon all rules? Do we present rules and regulations for our children's conduct, knowing they will probably defy and disobey? Do we follow our children everywhere they go so that we can be there to monitor all that they do? Do we wait to trap them, then punish them into compliance? None of the above is consistent with our new understanding of human beings and human behavior. Now we can understand that all that our children do is an attempt to follow their basic genetic instructions. What motivates our children to do the things they do is to behave in the world to have their quality world pictures become a reality. Although it may feel as if our children are doing things TO us, in reality they are doing things FOR themselves. What is happening is that the quality world picture of the child is different from the quality world picture of the parent. Our task is to figure out how to blend the two quality world pictures into one that is satisfactory to both child and parent.

This is easier said than done. A parent who believes that too much television time is not the best for her child has a very strong picture in her quality world of what she wants for her child. A parent who believes 14-year old girls should not wear makeup has a very strong picture in her quality world of the way she wants her daughter to look and behave. Each child has an equally strong picture in her quality world of what is right for herself related to television watching and makeup wearing.

We are the adults. As such, we certainly have greater power and control and can use powering and controlling behaviors in an attempt to power our children into getting what we want. But as I said earlier, this power is limited because our children eventually spend greater amounts of time out of our control. Ultimately, if we use this type of powering over behavior what may happen is that our children take the picture of us and their relationship with us out of their quality world because our relationship and behavior to them is no longer need-fulfilling. This is a condition we want to avoid.

As adults we have learned the sophisticated behavior of negotiating. (See Table 1, page 35.) With this tool we can negotiate with our children so that we can develop a compromise that will satisfy both the picture in our quality world as well as the picture in our child's quality world. Obviously, in order to do this we need to be aware of what our own picture is, and through conversation find out what our child's quality world picture is. Perhaps neither of us will get exactly what we want, but each of us can get a little of what we want. So, although as a parent we may have an idea of how much television we want our children to watch, we may have to negotiate with our child so he can get what he wants as well. Our child may want to watch unlimited television. So we may work out an arrangement where our child watches a limited amount of television on school nights but can watch as much as he wants on Saturday mornings until noon time. Our 14-year old daughter may think makeup is just fine, and as the parent we don't agree. So together we may need to arrive at a compromise of a little neutral lipstick with a small amount of mascara so both of us get a little of what we want.

What I am suggesting is that we accept that the pictures in our children's quality world are their ideal. We do not have to accept the total behavior that our child may want to act upon to get what it is he wants in his quality world. But we accept the ideas as his ideal. We share with our child what our picture is within the given situation. We work with our child to arrive at a compromise so that both child and parent get a little of what is wanted. The act of compromising and negotiating becomes a need-satisfying behavior that our child learns to help him successfully follow his instruction for power, freedom, love and belonging and perhaps even fun.

Table 1 describes compromise in detail. A parent may be happy to allow her child to participate in trick-or-treating during Halloween, but unhappy with the potential overconsumption of candy that may occur. Using negotiating and compromise, both parent and child explain to each other what they each want and the needs underlying these wants. Once they each understand this, then together they seek to arrive at a compromise that allows both to get what they need but may not include all of what each wanted.

The situation explained earlier, where a 12-year old wants to wear shorts to school and his mother thinks it is too cold may be resolved through negotiating around the underlying needs, rather than focusing only on the quality world pictures. The son wants to wear shorts, like his friends. The underlying needs, explained by the son, are belonging, being like his friends, freedom from the bulky winter clothes and anticipation of freedom from school. The mother wants her son to be physically comfortable enough to concentrate on his school work, with the underlying need being power for the mother. Being the mother of a child who is academically successful in school helps the mother meet her need for power. In the process of mother and son discussing this issue, mother may decide that her son will be more comfortable in school if he feels he fits in with his peers. The mother may decide to allow her son to wear shorts. If her son discovers he is too cold with such attire, then hopefully her son will dress for the temperature rather than the calendar in the future. Because the mother took the time to discuss this issue with her son, the mother realized that she was attempting to meet her needs by attempting to control and have power over her son's behavior. This could only happen through a conversation where both described not only their quality world pictures, but also their underlying needs.

TABLE 1

NEGOTIATING & COMPROMISE

HALLOWEEN CANDY

PARENT	CHILD
Quality world picture:	Quality world picture:
Child will eat one sweet per day	I can eat unlimited candy

NEGOTIATE

(Each explains reasons for quality world pictures)
(Look for underlying needs)

Maintain health	Enjoy the rewards of trick or treating
Good eating habits	Good taste of sweets
Survival	Fun and freedom needs

COMPROMISE

(Solution where each gets some of quality world picture)
(Both still able to meet needs)

Child can choose two treats per day:
one for snack time, one after lunch or dinner.
Snack time is chosen by child.

STAYING IN OUR CHILD'S QUALITY WORLD

As long as our children keep us and their relationship with us as a strong picture in their quality world we have the greatest chance to influence the pictures in their quality world. As long as we are a picture in our child's quality world, our child will want to work out compromises with us. Of all the genetic instructions we have, love and belonging are the most important instruction and need, even more important than survival. We are the first person in our children's lives with whom they meet this need. All that we do with, to and for our child should be directed by the love and belonging instruction. If our child keeps a picture of us as being a person with whom he is able to meet his need for love and belonging and is able to follow this instruction successfully, then we will remain a picture in our child's quality world. (We will also keep him in our quality world.) Staying in each other's quality world means our relationship is maintained. This is the most important thing in our lives together.

Negotiating with our child allows us to maintain our connected loving relationship with our child so that we remain a picture in his quality world. He may not necessarily be as delighted as he would be if he got all that he wanted. But then the parent isn't as satisfied as she would be if she got all that she wanted either. Getting a little of what we want while maintaining a workable and friendly relationship with our child should be the most important picture we constantly strive to keep, not only as a quality world ideal, but also as a reality.

THE BALANCING ACT

Learning when and how to negotiate as well as influence the pictures our child puts into his quality world is a balancing act that begins with the birth of our child. The amount of influence and impact we have on our child's adapting our ideas or rebelling against them varies with our child's age and stage. During the time when our child is most cooperative, focusing most of his behaviors on the fun and love instructions, our influence will be greatest in what our child accepts from our quality world to put into his, as long as these are need-fulfilling for him as well. During those times in his development when the competitive instructions of power and freedom are predominating his behaviors, he may listen to our ideas. But remember, he is focusing most of his behaviors on following his own instructions for power and freedom. So he may reject our ideas, not because they are not need-fulfilling, but because this is the time he is trying to demonstrate his power and freedom by not allowing us to influence him. In fact, we may be startled to learn later that what he rejected out of hand a few months before, he has now embraced as a good idea.

🏠   🏠   🏠   🏠

At age 9, David was struggling with asthma that interfered with his ability to enjoy life, especially during the winter months. This had been a part of our life since David was nine months old. I read everything I could find in the hope of helping him feel he had control over this debilitation. Visits to the allergy doctor revealed that David was allergic to nothing. Yet we lived with his daily struggle, no matter what the doctor's test results inaccurately revealed.

I had read a book where relaxation and visualization techniques were introduced to a child, helping the child feel as if he had the control and ability to relax himself through an asthma attack. Enthusiastically I introduced this idea to David. David was willing to try to follow my instructions as I talked him through the procedure. Afterward he told me the whole thing was dumb, and he wasn't going to do it. Disappointedly I resigned myself to continue searching for the support and help to share with David so that he would feel he was in charge of his own health and well-being.

When David was 14 years old, I watched him emerge from what I thought was an afternoon nap. He told me that he had just completed his relaxation and visualization process to help him avoid an oncoming asthma attack. Surprised, I asked him more about it.

"Oh, I've been doing this ever since you taught it to me years ago," he explained to me. "It really does help," he told me.

"I thought you thought it was stupid?" I asked.

"Well, that's what I told you," he said. "I didn't want you to think that your idea would work for me."

🏠   🏠   🏠   🏠

At the time I introduced these techniques to David, he was behaving to follow his power and freedom instructions. I was able to influence effective behaviors he added to his quality world. But because of the stage of development that he was in, he was not willing to let me know that my influence had been successful.

HOPES, DREAMS, ASPIRATIONS

"When we grow up, we're going to be professional wrestlers," my children explained to me at age five. "There are a couple of wrestlers now who are twin brothers. They will probably be ready to retire when we're old enough to take over."

Somehow, hearing this premonition did not fill my heart with joy. As their mother, I wanted my children to find fulfilling work when they reached adulthood. Picturing my sons as professional wrestlers was something I had never considered.

As they told me of their hearts' desire, I realized that my inability to picture this outcome was related to my own personal dismay that this possibility might become a reality. From where I sat, watching this Saturday morning entertainment, professional wrestlers resembled clowns more closely than athletes. Realizing there was plenty of time before they were old enough to make their choices, I decided to hold my tongue, saving my opinion until it might really count.

Twelve years later and several career dreams later, my children are still not sure how they want to spend their working lives. Professional wrestling is no longer their choice. (Thank goodness. I never had to say a word.) The glow and glory of this career choice tainted as they aged. For a time there were dreams of becoming professional athletes, either baseball players (for the Boston Red Sox, of course) or basketball players (for the Boston Celtics, of course). Each of their years spent in high school is working its own reality on the boys. They seem to be realizing that professional athletic options might only be available to a very extraordinary few. Their own individual assessments are that neither fits in that category.

My children were following their genetic instruction to be strong, powerful and recognized. Dreaming of how they could meet their need for power in their future led them to fantasize about their future career, as well as play act as wrestlers in the present. The genetic instruction for power drove them to behave. Dreaming and fantasizing were the behaviors they used to follow this instruction. Dreaming of being professional wrestlers was a creative idea of their own making. As children, aspiring to be professional athletes looked good. They could pretend and act out these fantasies, feeling powerful, strong and recognized right now, in the present.

As was already stated, quality world pictures are based on our actual experience in the world when one or more of our needs is satisfied. As well, when we develop an idea or a notion of what might be need-fulfilling, we place this possibility in our quality world. There are times when these notions may be unrealistic, seeming impossibilities. The wonderful part of the human experience is our ability to dream, aspire and hope even when the chances of any of these dreams, aspirations or hopes becoming a reality seem very small. I encourage all parents to foster their child's ability to develop these unrealistic possibilities. Who knows where they might lead.

There are some who will encourage parents to stifle their child's ability to imagine and dream. The reasoning is that a parent's job is to protect her child from future failure or disappointment. I strongly disagree. Just as my children changed their dream about striving to become professional wrestlers, so too most people, adults and children alike, squelch their own dreams too soon without actually attempting to have their dreams become a reality.

If people of all ages didn't dream, our world would be a very different place. Someone needs to aspire to become president of our country. Olympic athletes hope they will succeed in their given goals of competing in the Olympic Games, long before the year when teams are selected. Inventors dream of crazy new ways of solving problems. Thus inspired, the life of an American in the 1990s is very different from the life of an American in the 1890s, all because some inventors dreamed unrealistic ideas of how we could travel, heat and light our homes, and communicate with our neighbors, including our neighbors halfway around the globe. All of these people started out with some crazy pictures in their quality world of how they wanted to meet their needs and follow their genetic instructions. All successful people, no matter how we define success, have unrealistic goals, dreams and aspirations. It is because of these notions that people are motivated to behave. Some of these behaviors lead to some pretty amazing creations, including music, art, dance and theater.

I would strongly urge any parent to listen neutrally as her child tells of his hopes, dreams and aspirations, no matter what the age of the child. If our child wants these hopes, dreams, aspirations, or quality world pictures, enough, he will be motivated to behave in ways potentially to have his dreams come true. While he is aspiring toward these goals, the child himself may change his mind. In the striving, our child may discover another, more realistic quality world picture that is more readily and easily attainable. He still might never give up his impossible dream, though, and in the striving toward it will change the world as we know it. Unrealistic, potentially unattainable quality world pictures are the things that may contain the cure for cancer and solutions to world pollution, as well as the greatest symphony yet to be written.

SUMMARY

- Quality world pictures are total sensory, moving pictures in our consciousness that we believe will allow us to follow our genetic instructions successfully and meet our basic needs.
- Quality world pictures are based on actual experiences, as well as hoped for ideas or notions of what may be need-fulfilling.
- Our quality world pictures are not all of equal value. Those pictures that meet more than one need are of greater value than pictures that meet only one need. So a person's family may be a more important, more valued quality world picture than a person's car because a person can meet more needs with his family than with his car.
- Quality world pictures motivate all behavior, from birth to death. Genetic instructions drive us to behave. Quality world pictures motivate us to behave toward the quality world goals. Needs are general and generic. Quality world pictures are specific, individual and unique.
- Conflicts between people (parent and child, for instance), can now be understood as differing quality world

pictures. Negotiating is a skill and behavior that can help to resolve conflicts. Negotiating means both parties modify their individual quality world pictures to form a third quality world picture, one satisfying to both parties involved in the conflict.

- As parents, we can and do influence our children's quality world pictures. Because we are involved in each others' lives, we share experiences that are need-fulfilling, and we put these experiences in each of our quality worlds. Even with our influence and sharing, parents and children will still have differences in quality world pictures.

- Negotiating is an art that, when learned and used, allows parent and child to work out disagreements and con- flicts due to differing quality world pictures. Negotiating allows for the most important aspect of parenting: main- taining a loving relationship between parent and child. This means both parent and child maintain a picture of the other in their quality worlds.

- We must not squelch or stifle our child's hopes, dreams, and aspirations. These quality world pictures motivate be- havior. Our child may change his mind about these dreams as he grows and changes, or he may follow his dream and change the world!

Chapter Three
Behavior

ALL BEHAVIOR IS PURPOSEFUL

As humans, we are born with the instructions to go out in the world and meet our needs. This means that we need to behave in ways so that our picture of what we want (our quality world picture) matches what we perceive we are getting in the world. For instance, a person might begin feeling thirsty, being aware of his dry mouth and tight parched lips. Recognizing these feelings as indicating thirst, he begins to imagine a tall, sweating glass of ice water. The need for liquid comes from his genetic instruction for survival. Picturing a glass of ice water comes from his quality world. Other people might picture a glass of soda pop or a glass of iced tea. But our person has placed ice water into his quality world because through experiences in his life, he has found the most satisfaction for his genetic instruction of liquids to be drinking ice water. What this man does is to behave in the world, acting upon his quality world picture of a glass of ice water. Since he is home, it is easy enough for him to go into his kitchen, grab a glass from his cupboard, go to his freezer, collect some ice cubes from his ice tray, and fill the glass with water from the tap. He is so thirsty that he drinks the glass of water right down. He fills her glass with more water, waiting a few minutes this time for the water to begin to get cold and for the glass to begin to sweat. He has behaved successfully to have the quality world picture in his head match his perception of what he is experiencing in the world. His behavior is purposeful, effective and successful.

If this person were driving in his car on a long trip or on a summer hike, the kinds of behaviors might change in order for him to match successfully what he wants with what he is perceiving. He may need to stop at a convenience store and purchase bottled water or stop at a ranger's station and fill his canteen with water. All of his behaviors would still be purposeful, effective and successful.

Understanding that all behavior is purposeful can help to guide a parent as he lives and teaches his child. Whatever the behavior that a parent observes in his child, he can know that the child's behavior is purposeful. The purpose of ALL behavior is to attempt to match the picture that is in the child's head, her quality world picture, with what the child is perceiving in the world. As we discussed in the last chapter, these pictures are our quality world representations of how our genetic instructions will be satisfied. So the next time we see our child asking politely for a glass of juice, we can know that her behavior is an attempt to satisfy her genetic instruction of survival, ingesting liquids, that is represented in her quality world picture as juice.

LEARNING NEW BEHAVIORS

Probably this child did not begin her request for juice with the polite statement of "Juice please." Although this child may have had a picture of juice as the satisfying picture in her quality world to satisfy her need for survival for quite awhile, she behaved differently at different ages in her young life. As an infant, she cried because she did not know words. But her behavior was still quite purposeful. With perseverance and enough good guesses, a care-taker was able to identify that the cry was indicating the child's desire for juice. As the child began to learn language, crying, whining, grunting or pointing may have been the language the child used to indicate her need for something. Eventually, a parent may have begun to use the word "juice" to indicate that what was being given to the child had a name that could be spoken in words. Now the toddler made her request known by using the word "juice" over and over again until her request was met. The parent, delighted that the child knew what the word was, quickly fulfilled the child's request. But as the child grew older and her vocabulary increased, the parent began to insist that the child ask politely for "Juice please." So when the child forgot and reverted to her constant, loud, repeated request of "Juice! juice! juice!", the parent would correct the child by saying "Juice please" or asked the reminder question of "What is the magic word?" or "How do we ask for juice in our house?" What the parent is doing is teaching the child additional, more complicated behaviors to have the picture in the childs head match what she is perceiving she is getting in the world.

The parent has very definite pictures in his head of how he wants his daughter to behave. The picture in this fathers's head might be something like, "My daughter behaves in a cordial and polite way when making requests of people." This picture has evolved as well. His initial picture was "I want my baby to be happy and satisfied. I'll know that's how she feels because she won't be crying but will be smiling and cooing." This picture changes over time so that the father might begin to have a picture of "My daughter can talk with me and others in her world by using words." So when the child begins to declare her needs, using the word of "juice", the father perceives his daughter is behaving in the world consistent with the picture in the father's head. Once his daughter is talking more coherently, he begins to evolve the picture of "My daughter behaves and speaks in a cordial and polite way when making requests of me and other people." In a sense, the father is "shaping" the behavior of his child, based on the pictures in his head.

His daughter allows her behavior to be shaped because she loves and cares about her father. She has a picture in her quality world of her father being a person who helps her negotiate with the world to help her satisfy her basic needs, helping her to get in the world the pictures that match her quality world pictures. So when her father corrects her, and she says "Juice please" or something similar, she wants two things. She wants the juice, and she wants her father to continue to love and approve of her. Sometimes when a parent corrects a child's behavior, the child will not cooperate with the correction. Her need for whatever (in this case, juice) is greater at that moment than her need to keep her parent happy. Just as our thirsty man had an ideal picture of a glass of sweating ice water as being the most satisfying, he was thirsty enough that he didn't wait for the glass to begin sweating before he gulped down the water. Keeping this in mind might be helpful when we sometimes experience our child as willing to follow our correction, while other times she is not.

So far, we have been discussing all behaviors as purposeful when the behaviors are verbal requests and when the behaviors used are effective. However, there are times when behaviors are ineffective, and there are many more behaviors than just verbal. Let us take a look at these things one at a time.

EFFECTIVE AND INEFFECTIVE BEHAVIORS

As we've already begun to understand, all behavior is purposeful. The purpose for all behavior is to attempt to have the quality world pictures in our head become a reality in the world. When the behaviors we use match what we want and what we perceive we are getting, we call that success, satisfaction and pleasure. We have learned effective behaviors. We remember these behaviors and store them in our memory to be used again in the future for similar circumstances, so that we will have success, satisfaction and pleasure in the future.

Sometimes, however, we have a picture in our head of what we want, we behave in the world, and we do not get what we want. We call this dissatisfaction, frustration, pain. We continue to behave in an attempt to get what we want, but our behaviors may continue to be ineffective. That is, we still don't get a match between what we want and what we are experiencing. At this point we may use a wide variety of behaviors, even behaviors we know probably won't work, but we may not take the time to evaluate the potential success of these behaviors. We just want what we want. As in the previous example, the child may continue to scream "Juice, juice, juice" even though she may know that screaming will probably not get her what she wants. After a period of time if the screaming still doesn't work, she may resort to other behaviors of whining, crying, wailing and throwing herself on the floor. Somewhere in her experience, she probably knows that crying, wailing and throwing herself around will not increase the chances she will effectively get what she wants, but she doesn't take the time to evaluate the effectiveness of her behavior. She only knows she wants the pain of not having what she wants to go away. So she uses the most effective behaviors available to her at the time even though these behaviors are not effective enough to get her what she wants.

Another example from our own experience might help to clarify effective versus ineffective behaviors. Let's imagine that we have an important engagement away from our office or home. We know how long it will take to get from point A to point B. Because of the importance of this appointment, our intention is to leave early so that we are sure to be there on time. It is one of those days where we can't get out of our own way. So we end up leaving with exactly enough time to get to our engagement on time. As we drive along, obeying the speed limit, we are feeling confident that we will be there as scheduled. Continuing along our way, on the two-lane highway, we are suddenly cut off by a very slow driver pulling out in front of us. It is now becoming increasingly apparent to us that if we continue at this rate, we will be late for our appointment.

We perceive a large gap between what we want, our quality world picture of being on time for our appointment, and what is happening, a slow driver causing us to be late. We feel this difference as frustration and begin to behave in ways to change the driver in front of us, in an attempt to get what we want effectively. Some of the behaviors people have been known to use are swearing, flashing lights, flashing various fingers at the driver in front of them, tail-gating, attempting to pass, or slowing down so there is a large gap between them and the driver in front of them and then speeding up right on the bumper of the car in front of them. Generally speaking, these behaviors are not very effective. Occasionally these behaviors are successful, though, or people wouldn't keep them in their memory as behaviors to try. Often what results is that the driver in front of them slows down instead of speeding up or moving over so they can pass.

Obviously these behaviors are not effective. In fact, sometimes they are even more frustrating to what we wanted in the first place, but we didn't take the time to evaluate the effectiveness of our behaviors before we tried them. We were concentrating on trying to get to our engagement on time. We were aware that the driver in front of us was potentially interfering with what we wanted, so we behaved in purposeful ways to get what we wanted, choosing the most effective behaviors available to us at the time even though these behaviors were all ineffective.

As parents read this scenario, they can probably think of alternative behaviors that would be more effective in these circumstances, including the behavior of deciding to be late for their appointment as being a better alternative than getting themselves or someone else killed trying to be there on time. But when we are in the midst of an episode like the above, it is harder to use the behavior of keeping calm and thinking logically.

Our job, as parents, is to help our children learn the most effective behaviors possible, to increase the chance they will get what they want, no matter how frustrated or unsatisfied they may be. Understanding that behaviors, whether effective or ineffective, are not the problem, can be helpful. The problem, from the child's perspective, is she is not getting what she wants. She is using all the behaviors available to her at the time, and these behavioral choices may be ineffective. But she doesn't care about effective or ineffective. All she cares about is getting what she wants. She may not care initially whether the new behaviors are acceptable or unacceptable to us. Again, all she cares about is getting what she wants. We may have a problem with the behaviors our child chooses because her behaviors may be different from the pictures in our quality world of how we want our child to behave. Our job, as parents, is to help our child learn more effective behaviors that are consistent with the pictures in our quality world to help her get what she wants. She will be very willing to learn and use different behaviors, as long as they are effective in helping her get what she wants.

TEACHING EFFECTIVE BEHAVIORS

Susan's three-year old son, Johnnie, and her five-year old daughter, Mary, are playing in the den. The two are aware of the other's presence in the room, but they are not playing together. Susan is close by in the kitchen, preparing dinner for the family. Suddenly the quiet individual activities of the three are interrupted by a large scream followed by Johnnie's crying. When Susan goes into the den to investigate what has happened, Mary explains to her mother that she had been playing with the blocks, building a castle for her horses to live in, when Johnnie came over, grabbing a block in each hand and knocking down the structure. Mary, furious for the interruption and the damage, grabbed the blocks back and in the process, knocked Johnnie over.

Dealing with each child in turn, Susan finds out what Mary wants: her blocks so that she can build her castle and the assurance that her structure will not be demolished in the process of her game. Susan asks Mary how she went about achieving her goal. Mary explained that she grabbed the blocks.

"Did you get what you wanted?" Susan asks Mary.

"Kind of," Mary replies.

"How?" Susan asks.

"I've got the blocks." Mary explains. "But now Johnnie is screaming mad, and you're in here. I probably won't be able to play with the blocks any more without Johnnie coming over all the time and stealing them." Mary has enough experience with her brother to know that his behavior of block grabbing will probably continue.

"What do you think Johnnie wants?" Susan asks Mary.

"To ruin my game," Mary replies honestly.

Susan persists. "It might feel like that. But if you had to guess what Johnnie really wants besides making you unhappy, what would you guess?"

"Maybe he wants to play with the blocks," Mary guesses.

"I would guess that, too," says Susan. "He probably saw how much fun you were having with the blocks and decided he wanted to have that kind of fun, too. I'm going to talk with Johnnie in just a minute. If we find out that our guess of Johnnie's wanting to play with the blocks is right, how do you think we could work this out so you can get what you want and Johnnie can get what he wants?"

"I guess I could let him have some of the blocks to play with. But I don't want him helping me to build my castle, if that's what he wants. He'll only mess things up," Mary replies.

"Okay. Now I know what you want and what idea you have about how we can work this out so you can get what you want and Johnnie can get what he wants. What did you want when you grabbed the blocks back from Johnnie and knocked him down?" Susan continues.

"I wanted my blocks back," Mary explains the obvious to her mother.

"So you got what you wanted, but what about Johnnie?"

"Oh, he wasn't really hurt. He's just acting like a cry baby," Mary says defensively.

"Hmm. Can you think of another way you could have gotten what you wanted without hurting Johnnie? Either hurting him physically or hurting his feelings?" Susan is not going to let Mary off the hook here.

"Yes. I guess I should have come to you and asked for help."

"Good. Do you think you can do that in the future, Mary? At times when you feel like hurting your brother, before you do, come ask me for help," Susan explains.

"I didn't mean to hurt him. I just wanted my blocks back," Mary says.

"I know, Mary. You were trying to get what you wanted. But the way you went about it did hurt Johnnie. Do you see what I mean?" Susan asks. Mary nods. "Let me talk with Johnnie for a little bit, and I'll let you know what happens."

Now Susan turns her attention to Johnnie, who has been listening to his mother and sister's conversation while pushing a toy car around the area.

"Johnnie, what did you want when you came over to Mary's castle?"

"The blocks," Johnnie replies, confirming Susan's and Mary's hunch.

"How did you go about getting what you wanted?" Susan continues.

"I took the blocks," Johnnie explains.

"What happened when you took the blocks?" Susan asks.

"Mary pushed me down. I cried," Johnnie says.

"Mary didn't just push you down for no reason though, did she Johnnie? When you took the blocks, what happened to Mary's castle?" Susan asks.

"The castle fell down and broke," Johnnie says.

"That's right, Johnnie. Mary had worked hard to build her castle so she could put her horses in it. When you took the blocks, you broke up what she was doing. I don't think you meant to upset Mary. I think you just wanted the blocks, to play with. Am I right?" At this stage, Susan does a lot more of the work and the talking, but she is teaching Johnnie some important lessons about how he can get what he wants and not interfere with other people, namely his sister, from getting what she wants.

"I want to play with blocks, too," Johnnie explains.

"How do you think you could get some blocks to play with, without hurting Mary or breaking up what she is doing?" Susan asks.

Johnnie concentrates very hard. His mother tries to help him out. *"Remember, we've talked about how we can get things from other people at our house, besides just taking what we want?"*

"Ask!" Johnnie says, delighted he has found an answer.

"That's right Johnnie. We ask. Would you still like to play with the blocks?" Susan asks. Johnnie nods. *"How are you going to try to get some?"*

Johnnie walks over to his sister and says, *"Mary I want blocks."*

Mary puts conditions on accommodating his request. *"I'll give you these five blocks Johnnie, but you need to play over there, far away from me and my castle and horses."*

Johnnie agrees, takes his five blocks to another part of the room, along with his car, and starts building something of his own.

All three of the people in this scenario had different pictures in their heads of what they wanted. Susan wanted the freedom to prepare a meal while her children entertained themselves peacefully. Mary wanted her blocks and her horses and the freedom to build her dreams without interference. Johnnie wanted to play with blocks and have as much fun as his sister seemed to be having. Because Johnnie is only three and hasn't learned the effective and sophisticated behavior of negotiating, he used a tried and true behavior of grabbing. At least in this scene, he didn't want to annoy or hurt his sister. He just wanted some blocks. When taught an alternative behavior to help him get what he wanted, he was more than willing to use it. But Susan will probably need to remind and repeat her instructions to Johnnie more than a few times before he learns it. Mary may not always be in such an accommodating mood either. Luckily, today she was. Although Johnnie is younger and just learning about living and playing in a family, Mary has two more years' experience with this type of process, so she is more familiar with how her mother helps her to work things out.

We can also see from this scene that the personal behaviors were not the problem for any of the individuals. The problem was that none of these people were getting what they each wanted. Mary's behavior of grabbing her blocks back and knocking her brother down in the process was not her problem. For her, the problem was that she had lost two blocks and her castle had been knocked over. Johnnie's behavior was not a problem for him. Not having any blocks to play with was his problem. Because these two live and play together, they need to learn how to get what each one wants without interfering with what the other person wants.

The mother's job in this case was to help her children learn how to do this, ultimately helping her get what she wants. Her immediate desire of continuing to prepare a family meal uninterrupted may have been temporarily side-tracked. Because she is the adult, her job is to look for the longer term goal, the more valued quality world picture of her children learning to work things out with each other, while temporarily putting her immediate goal aside.

ALL BEHAVIOR
IS TOTAL

Finally, let's turn our attention to understanding the concept of behavior. This idea may not be as obvious as you think. Typically, when people hear the term behavior, what comes to mind is action. Johnnie was grabbing, crying and talking. When I use the word behavior I mean more than just action. All behavior has four component parts that make up a person's total behavior. Action is part of it. The three other parts are thinking, feeling and physiology. Although we describe behavior by the most obvious component part, all four are occurring simultaneously. So while Mary was engaged in the action of castle-building, she was thinking about the story in her head of horses living in a castle, flying to distant lands and returning to their castle home. She was feeling excited and brave, as well as productive as she built a home for her horses. The physiological component of her behavior can be measured with tests like counting her heartbeat or her breaths or taking her temperature, although under ordinary circumstances this would never be done. The physiological component of her behavior keeps her physical body functioning so she can accomplish the task before her. Anyone watching Mary's behavior would describe it by the most apparent component. We would say that Mary is playing, using her fantasy and imagination, indicating the acting and thinking components of her behavior. But all four components are occurring simultaneously and are in accord with one another.

All of us have had the experience of reading a good murder mystery or watching a thriller movie. Although the acting component of our behavior may be rather passive, in that we are watching or reading, our thinking is riveted along with the plot. Our feelings of fear and tension are also molded by the plot. If anyone were to take blood chemistries during the most frightening parts of the movie or book, our levels of adrenaline would be elevated. All four components of our behavior are occurring simultaneously, and all are in alignment with one another.

So when we talk about all behavior being purposeful, we mean all four components of our behavior: the acting, the thinking, the feeling and the physiology. When a baby sits on the floor looking up at her father with her arms outstretched toward her father, she is thinking, "I want Daddy to hold me; I want to feel close to Dad," and her physiology is craving the support and warmth of her father's hold. When a two-year old throws herself on the floor, kicking and flailing her arms about, screaming and crying her thoughts out loud, "NO, no, no," feeling angry and frustrated while her body is tight and tense, she is communicating some quality world picture that is unsatisfied in her life.

Our job, as parents, is to learn to read all components of our child's behavior and help her learn how to get what it is that she wants effectively. Sometimes we can listen to the verbal requests, the action of asking. Sometimes we need to guess, based on other behavioral components that we see and hear. Based on our guesses, we begin to put words to the possibilities of the purpose of her behaviors and ask our child if the guess is accurate. Then we can begin to teach our child to use words to ask for what it is that she wants.

CHANGING BEHAVIOR

Because all behavior is total, comprised of all four behavioral components, if we change one behavioral component, all the others will change as well. Remember, we said that all four components are in accord with each other and are occurring simultaneously. So change one and the others also change.

Take the changes that occur when we change a walking stride to a jogging or running stride. The action initially is walking, while our thinking might be observations of our surroundings, our feeling might be contentment, and our physiology would be a heart rate of 82 beats per minute, respiration of 20 respirations per minute, and so forth. Now we change our stride to a slow run or jog. We have only changed one component, the acting component. But all the other components change simultaneously. Our thoughts might be about how good it feels to stretch our legs and swing our arms. Or perhaps we begin to think that this feels lousy, wondering how much longer we need to keep running. Our feelings might change to increased pleasure or perhaps to displeasure. And our physiological changes would be increased heart rate, increased respiration, as well as increased body temperature, as we will eventually begin to perspire. All we have done is to change one behavioral component, but all the others changed simultaneously because all behavior is total and interconnected.

The hardest behavioral components to change are the feeling and and the physiology components. We can test this for ourselves. While we sit and read this book, we tell ourselves to begin to perspire, then to stop perspiring; to feel angry, then to feel happy; to think about the color green, to think about the last meal we ate. Then we tell ourselves to turn this book upside-down. Of all the things we asked ourselves to do, which was the easiest to change? For most people the answer is change from thinking about green to the last meal eaten, and to turn the book upside-down. These are the acting and thinking components of behavior. When you changed these components, the other components changed as well because all behavior is total and interconnected. Some of us may have attempted to perspire by imagining or THINKING of being some place very hot. Those of us who attempted to feel angry tried by THINKING of the last argument we had with someone or felt happy by THINKING of some activity we enjoy doing. It is through the thinking component that we attempted to change the physiological or feeling components of behavior. If we hadn't been reading this book, we also might have tried to change either the physiological or feeling component through some kind of action. Because we have the most arbitrary control over the acting and thinking components, we can use this information to help us change our behaviors.

Changing behavior is never easy. If it were, all of us would have kept every New Year's resolution we ever made. There are times, however, when all of us are trying to make some kind of behavioral change. Understanding that all behavior is total, and that the behavioral components we have the most control over are the acting and thinking components, can aid us as we try to make these behavioral changes. Knowing and using this information can also help us when our children ask us to help them make behavioral changes.

＊　　＊　　＊　　＊

A father is grocery shopping for a few items with his seven-year old daughter. He is anxious to get through the store as quickly as possible and then move on to other errands he has planned for his Saturday morning. Jenny is happy to be running errands with her father.

In the cereal aisle, Jenny asks her father to buy a box of Fruit Loops. He denies the request. In the pasta aisle, she requests the colored macaroni. He says no, this time reminding her that they are there only to purchase the things on their list. In the bread aisle, she approaches her father with a jar containing both peanut butter and jelly. Again he denies her request, this time frustration showing in the tone of his voice.

As they approach the checkout area, Jenny runs ahead to inspect all the wonderful items she regards as great treasures that grocery stores seem to place strategically at children's eye level. Running back to her father, she begins to tell him all the things she thinks they need to add to their carriage for purchase. Her father stops mid-stride, just shy of reaching the checkout area. He bends down so that he is eye level with Jenny. He opens his arms, asking her for a big hug. During their embrace, he tells Jenny how much he loves her, how glad he is that she is helping him and keeping him company while they run errands together. He asks her if she will help him when they get to the cashier by placing items from their carriage onto the belt for checkout. Happily, Jenny agrees.

Purchases made, they walk to the car together. Father tells Jenny where they are going next, what the items are that they are looking to buy, and asks her if she will be in charge of finding one specific item.

＊　　＊　　＊　　＊

In this scene, father had a specific picture in his head of going into and out of the grocery store as quickly as possible. With every request that Jenny made of what he considered unnecessary items, he was feeling more and more short-tempered and angry. At her final request, the father finally changed his behavior from dismissal and denial. He changed his action to embracing, loving and including his daughter in the plans and successful completion of their morning tasks. He changed the thinking component of his behavior from, "I need to get in and out of here as quickly as possible," to "How can I help Jenny help me? How can I include her in our errands?" He changed the acting component from walking up and down the aisles looking for what he wanted to purchase while offhandedly denying Jenny's request, to hugging her, telling her he loved her, and asking for her help through her active participation. As a result of changing his thinking and acting components, his feelings changed from frustration and annoyance to happy, loving feelings. He still didn't love the errands he was doing, but he loved spending time with his daughter, instead of feeling annoyed by her interference.

SUMMARY

- We behave in the world to get what we want. All behavior is purposeful. The purpose of all behavior is to get what we want (the picture in our quality world) to meet our needs effectively and follow our genetic instructions.
- A parent's job is to help his child learn new behaviors to help her get what she wants. These new behaviors include learning language and asking for what she wants.
- Correcting our children's behavior to a different, more effective and acceptable behavior is not always heeded by our children. All behavior is purposeful, and the child may have a stronger urge to get what she wants than the urge to listen and adjust to our correction.
- Some purposeful behaviors are effective, getting us what we want. Some purposeful behaviors are ineffective, not getting us what we want. A parent's job is to help the child learn effective behaviors.
- All behavior is comprised of four component parts: acting, thinking, feeling and physiology. All four components occur simultaneously. We name behavior by the most apparent component: playing (acting), studying (thinking), being angry (feeling), crying (physiology).

- Acting and thinking are the components that are the easiest to change because it is these two components over which we have the most arbitrary control. When attempting to change behavior, we should work to change the acting and the thinking components for the greatest success in changing behavior.

Chapter Four
Self-Evaluating

CHANGING DISCOMFORT TO COMFORT

Have you ever wondered how we know it's time to go to bed or time to eat? How is it we know when we need to put a sweater on or to take one off? How do we know when to get a glass of water to quench our thirst or when we need to go to the bathroom to empty our bladders? What do all of these things have in common? In each instance we get an internal feeling or signal that urges us to behave to increase our sense of comfort and satisfaction. All of these signals come from a self-regulating mechanism that allows us to self-evaluate and know that we need to do something to change our discomfort back to a sense of comfort. Sometimes this feeling or signal is stronger than other times. What these internal feelings have in common is that they are all experienced as an urge to behave.

We are now coming to understand the full system of how our brains function, with self-evaluation being the final tool. We are all born with the amazing ability to self-evaluate. Self-evaluation is the self-regulating process that enables us to know when the world is as we want it to be or to know when things are not the way we want. When we experience the world differently from what we want, we behave in an attempt to change the world so that it more closely matches our ideal quality world picture of what we want.

Let's examine room temperature as our first example. Each of us has a specific temperature that feels ideal for us. This perfect temperature is our quality world picture of the level of heat and coolness we want in our environment. Most of us are probably not even aware of what this temperature is, we just know it is right when we feel it. Each of us has an ideal room temperature in which we like to live and operate.

Remember, this ideal is the picture that is in our quality world. It is individual and unique for each of us. Perhaps others that we live and work with have a different ideal temperature. This can result in discussions and compromises as co-workers or family members negotiate the setting of the thermostat in a shared office or in the house.

When the temperature in our environment rises too far above or falls too far below our ideal temperature, we act. Before we act by taking our jackets off or putting a sweater on, there is a signal generated from our self-regulating system of self-evaluation that lets us know that the temperature we want is different from the temperature we are experiencing. All of the behaviors which we could choose to change the room back to the ideal room temperature are purposeful. The purpose of these behaviors is to return our environment to our ideal comfort temperature level. But before we choose any of these actions, we first self-evaluate that the temperature in the room is different from the temperature we want. Our marvelous ability to self-evaluate is what informs us that the temperature is different from what we want.

LEARNING TO SURVIVE AND MORE

This self-regulating system, called self-evaluation, allows us to determine when we need to go to the bathroom, eat when we are hungry, and drink when we are thirsty, as well as evaluate when our behavior needs modification and correction when learning to walk, spell, create an artistic project or write a creative short story. Originally this function was probably only biological. That is, we needed to know when what we were doing was putting our survival at risk. If we were exposed to cold temperatures for too long, we needed to be alerted to this information so that we would act to get to warmer surroundings before we froze to death. This self-regulating system still works to our advantage in terms of survival, but as we have mentioned before, there is much more to living than just survival. Our job, as parents and guardians, is to help our children pay attention to their self-evaluations and use this information to make effective choices as they live, learn, grow and mature.

Simply put, self-evaluation is the process of comparing what we want with what we are getting. When we evaluate that what we want is the same as what we are getting, we feel pleasure, satisfaction and comfort. When we evaluate that what we want is different from what we are getting, we feel dissatisfaction, pain and experience an urge to behave. We feel driven to behave in the world to change the world into what we want.

BEGINNING AT BIRTH

When we self-evaluate that the world we are experiencing is different from our quality world, we are driven to behave. This process begins at birth. Another example may help.

Let's imagine the world of a growing fetus in utero. Sounds exist but are muted and muffled except for the strong continuous rhythm of mother's heartbeat. Our world is dark, with a slight amount of dim light. The temperature is just right, not too cold nor too hot. There is no such thing as hunger. The amount of space in our world is ever decreasing until, in the last few weeks before birth, we are very tightly cramped in our space. This is the only environment we have ever known, and it is perfect. We hold onto this sensory picture in our quality world of how we want our environment: just as it has been.

Immediately after birth we experience the world outside of our mother's womb. Loud sounds attack us. Bright lights assault our eyes. We are very cold. There is more space to move our arms and legs than we ever imagined. What we are experiencing is very different from what we have experienced up to this point of our very short lives.

A baby's initial experience of the world immediately after birth is very different from the muted, quiet, protected, increasingly cramped world in utero. As soon as a baby is born, he self-evaluates that what he wants from his environment and what he is experiencing are two, very different things. This new world is not welcomed by the baby. The baby has a strong urge to behave in an attempt to change the world back to the way it was. Many newborn babies cry (a behavior) to accomplish this task. These are not woeful, sad cries, but mad, angry wails, demanding the world get back to the way it should be! Eventually, after the medical staff have tested, weighed, measured and cleaned the baby, they finally tightly swaddle the baby in a receiving blanket and return the baby, face down, to the mother's chest. The miracle we see next is that the newborn baby quiets down and falls asleep. The baby has once again self-evaluated. Now what he wants the world to be like is finally what he is getting. That is, he is experiencing a tightly restricted space with an ever present pounding of mother's heartbeat. Because baby is getting what he wants, he has no urge to behave. So he falls asleep to rest after his exhausting birth experience.

CONTINUOUS SELF-EVALUATION

This quiet sleep doesn't last too long because eventually the baby receives another urge to behave. He becomes aware that the feeling he wants to have in his tummy is different from what he is experiencing. So his self-evaluate of this difference urges him to behave. He begins wailing and crying all over again, screaming at the world to change back to what he wants. Through trial and error, a care-giver finally figures out that the baby is hungry, and the baby is put to the breast or given a bottle.

In the beginning of our child's life, he is in touch with his self-regulating, self-evaluating system by feelings of pain or comfort. When a baby feels pain in his stomach because there is not enough food, he begins to cry, thus alerting the care-giver that something needs to be done for the child. Eventually the care-giver figures out what the child wants, so the child is fed. When the child has had enough food, the feeling of satiation, satisfaction and fullness is experienced by the infant, so the baby stops eating. He has a sensory picture of the feeling he wants in his tummy and because he is experiencing what he wants, he stops behaving, stops eating. The care-giver determines the baby has had enough because the child stops eating.

Sometimes we may believe that the child has not had enough to eat. We may burp the baby, thus eliminating air in his stomach that we believe may be giving the child the false impression of fullness. Perhaps the baby does experience fullness, but some of that fullness may be air expansion, not food satisfaction. After the baby burps, we attempt to feed the child more. If the baby still experiences fullness and satisfaction, the child will not continue to eat. His self-evaluative system is telling him that enough is enough. No matter what the adult care-giver believes about the amount of food the child should be eating, the child will not continue to eat when he is full and satisfied. Self-regulation and self-evaluation rule this child's behavior.

Miracle, isn't it? We are born with a self-regulating system that urges us to behave when the world we are experiencing is different from the world we want, and lets us know when we are satisfied. Our self-evaluation informs us when the world we want is the same as the world we are experiencing, so we stop behaving. We are finally satisfied that what we want is what we are getting, so we have no urge to behave.

Initially the newborn does not feel the self-regulating system. All the newborn feels is pain. He is not even aware of an urge to behave. He just cries, communicating to those in his immediate surroundings that he is in pain and not happy. So the care-givers act to change the world to increase the baby's comfort.

The care-givers may not be able to describe their own self-evaluating system either. As parents, we have a picture in our head that we want our child to be comfortable and satisfied. Crying indicates to us that our baby is unhappy. Our self-evaluation of what we want and what we are getting drives us to behave to change the baby's world so that he will stop crying. This indicates to us that the baby is no longer unhappy, so we get what we want, a comfortable and satisfied baby. The baby's urge to cry as well as our own urge to change the world the baby is experiencing so he will stop crying, are based on the self-regulating system in each of us to self-evaluate.

THINKING

Initially this self-regulating system is not part of what we would call the conscious, thinking part of a newborn's brain. As we grow and mature, our ability to think consciously, with greater awareness of our thoughts, increases. This includes our ability to be conscious of our self-evaluations. Whether we help our children learn this part of their brain or not, the process of self-evaluation exists for all humans. As parents, we can help our children learn about this internal process, helping them learn how to use their self-evaluation to learn more effective ways to live their lives.

As our child gets older, we can help him learn to increase his awareness of the self-evaluating process to help him learn increasingly difficult and complicated behaviors. He can learn to use self-evaluation to increase the effectiveness of his behaviors, self-evaluating the effectiveness or ineffectiveness of his behavior in helping him get what he wants.

We are all born knowing how to do a limited number of things. Babies are born knowing how to suck and cry, for instance, increasing their chances of survival. If a baby is going to mature and be able to live independently, however, there are greater and increasingly more complicated behaviors that must be learned. Self-evaluation facilitates this learning.

A newborn does not stop to think that his new world is different from what he wants. He experiences this difference as pain and wails in an attempt to get rid of the pain. Crying doesn't feel like a purposeful choice to behave to change the pain back into the comfort he wants. Yet his behavior is purposeful.

As an infant becomes more aware of the world and himself in the world, he becomes increasingly aware that he has some effect on his world. He begins to learn that smiling and laughing are behaviors that result in his mother's smiling and laughing with him. This feels good. He is developing pictures in his quality world that he wants his mother to be with him, to laugh and smile with him because it meets his need for love and belonging. He is beginning to discover that his own smiling and laughing results in his mother's smiling and laughing. Although he is still not aware of what we would call the effect that his behavior is causing, he is certainly using his self-evaluation to determine if he is getting what he wants.

After only a few months, babies have learned a number of behaviors that they can use to try to change the world into what they want. The baby's behavior becomes more intentional as well as purposeful. If baby is wanting more in his environment to explore, he will try crying, then salivating, then rocking, then arm and leg flailing in an attempt to get something into his mouth to suck and explore. With each behavior he evaluates his success and satisfaction. If he still doesn't get what he wants, he will change to another of the behaviors he has learned, to see if he can get the satisfaction that he wants. As parents, we do not need to teach this to our children. This is part of what they are born already knowing.

LEARNING COMPLICATED BEHAVIORS

The self-evaluation process allows our child to learn the complicated behavior of becoming toilet trained. As adults, each of us has a sensory picture in our head of how we want our bladders and bowels to feel in order for us to feel comfortable. When our bladders and bowels begin to fill up, our body sends us a signal that we are out of our physiological comfort zone. Eventually this self-evaluation signal gets loud enough so that we act and visit the bathroom to empty our bladders and bowels, thus returning our bodies to the bladder and bowel comfort zone.

Children have the same experience, but because they wear diapers, when their body gives them the signal that their bladders and bowels are getting too full for comfort, they relieve themselves immediately into the diaper. Some, but not all children, experience a soiled diaper as an uncomfortable signal and may begin to fuss or cry to let the care-giver know that diapers need changing.

Eventually children grow old enough that we want to begin to teach them to use a toilet instead of a diaper to relieve themselves. Eventually our child begins to have a similar picture in his head as well (although often the timing of this may be later for the child than for the adult). Our job, as the adults is to teach our children to pay attention when their bladders and bowels send them a signal. Helping children learn what a small signal feels like helps them to have success.

At first this means asking our child to pay attention to how he feels when his bladder is empty. We don't need to do more than ask. After about an hour, we again ask our child to pay attention to how his bladder feels. Does it feel full? Does the feeling he has feel different from how good he feels when his bladder is empty. Does he feel the urge to urinate? This feeling to urinate, to behave, is coming from his self-evaluation. His full bladder feels different from his empty bladder. He wants the empty feeling because it is a more comfortable feeling. This difference is felt as an urge to behave. This is the time to visit the toilet. (For some children learning to control bowel movements intentionally may be better understood and learned before bladder control, but the idea is the same.)

We are asking our child to be conscious, aware of the built-in quality world pictures and accompanying self-evaluation process. When our child misses the early signal and has an accident, we can talk to our child about what the signal felt like, how strong and long it was, and what happened when the child ignored the signal for too long. Just before the urge to urinate is a feeling that what we want and what we are experiencing are not the same. Teaching our child to learn to tune into his system, becoming aware of a difference between what he wants and what he perceives he is getting, enables him to be aware of his self-evaluation and be more purposeful and intentional about his behavior.

This same process applies not only to toilet training, but all aspects of our life and our child's life. If we slow down and become conscious of our self-evaluation, we have the time and opportunity to choose the most effective behaviors to help us change the world to be the way we want it to be. Thus, the behaviors we use to act upon the world to change it do not need to be automatic responses.

A 30-year old mother does not need to hit her child when her child automatically hits her. For a four-year old child, the ability to choose something other than hitting back may not feel like a choice the child can make. But the mother has matured enough to be aware of the difference between what she wants, her child to hug her, and what she is getting, her child hitting her. The mother can decide on more effective ways to handle this situation when first she becomes aware of her self-evaluation signal that is telling her that what she is getting from her son is different from what she wants. Although the mother may experience a strong urge to hit her son back, the mother realizes that this strong urge is just that, an urge to behave to change her son's behavior. Because the mother has increased her awareness of her signal, she can slow down and evaluate the variety of behaviors available to her to help get the world to be the way she wants.

The mother's self-evaluation is that hitting her son will not help her have a loving, hugging relationship with her son. So, based upon this self-evaluation, the mother decides not to hit her son. The mother decides that despite her strong urge to act in some way, she will choose to think instead. The mother thinks to herself that her son is feeling upset and frustrated. The mother is aware that these feelings of upset and hitting indicate that her son wants something he is not getting and he is using hitting in an attempt to change the world. The mother decides to talk with her son to see if she can help her son choose a more effective behavior to help him get what he wants.

Using the same process as she did for toilet training, the mother asks her son what he wants, what he perceives he is getting now, and what the feeling was just before he hit. Was the son aware of his urge to hit? Was the son aware of some feeling just before he was aware of wanting to hit? The feeling that occurred just before the son hit was the son's self-evaluation that what he was getting was different from what he wanted. Although the son might not be able to answer his mother's questions right away, his mother continues to ask this question throughout the day at other times when the son may not be getting what he wants. Eventually the son will learn what his small, internal, self-evaluation signal feels like. Being aware of the signal will allow the son to slow down so that he can then choose from a variety of behaviors that may increase the chance that he can effectively change the world to be closer to the son's quality world picture.

GETTING WHAT WE WANT

We experience an internal signal or feeling when we self-evaluate that what we want and what we are getting are a match. This signal may be harder to recognize, however, because generally there is no feeling or urge to behave accompanying the signal. You may not even be aware when the temperature in the room is just what you want it to be. You have no urge to change the temperature. We need to focus not only on the signal or feelings we get when our self-evaluation indicates that the world is different from what we want. We also need to focus on the signal or feeling we get when we experience a match. Recognizing this signal of comfort, pleasure and satisfaction is very important, even if it is difficult to recognize.

Our brain is set up to give us a louder, stronger, more discomforting signal when we self-evaluate that what we want and what we are getting are different. An urge to behave based on a mismatching self-evaluation drives us to behave in ways that will increase our chance of surviving. But the matching feelings that come from self-evaluation allow us to learn effective behaviors, recognizing when our quality world picture is what we are presently getting in the world. So we must go out of our way to pay attention and increase our awareness when we receive pleasurable, satisfying signals that let us know the world and the people in it are just as we want.

Taking the time to pay attention to the feeling and signal that accompany a match between what we want and what we are experiencing allows us to experience the fullness, richness and pleasures in our life. It also allows us to learn that some behaviors are more effective than others. "Taking time to smell the roses" means paying attention to when our lives are the way we want them to be, no matter how small the match. If we pay attention to the moments when we self-evaluate a match between what we want and what we are getting, we can consciously learn and then remember the effective behaviors that made the match possible.

As parents, we need to pay attention to when our children are behaving just as we want them to, not only when our children are misbehaving. This allows us to relish in the pleasures and satisfaction that our children bring to our lives. A conscious awareness that politely asking our son to remove his hat at the dinner table resulted in his doing so more effectively than giving him a stern and disapproving look, allows us to remember to use this effective behavior if there is a next time, to help us get what we want.

EFFECTIVE VS. INEFFECTIVE BEHAVIORS

As we discussed in the previous chapter, the drive or urge to behave is not specific in terms of HOW we behave. All we know is that we must do something, attempting to change the world into what we want. Self-evaluation not only urges us to behave, it also allows us to decide, evaluate and judge how we will behave.

If the temperature in my house is too cold, that is colder than the ideal quality world picture I have of the most comfortable temperature I want my house to be, I am driven to behave in order to warm the house. Among the behaviors I could choose to warm the house includes setting the house on fire. This certainly would increase the temperature. By self-evaluating ahead of this action, I can determine that this action would get me more than I want. Yes, the temperature would increase, but probably would increase in the opposite direction to the point of discomfort. Not only would I then have a house that is too hot, eventually I would have no house at all!

So self-evaluating not only allows us to compare what we want the world to be like with how the world is, it also allows us to compare the effectiveness or ineffectiveness of our behavioral choices in regulating and changing the world to match our ideal quality world picture. This process allows us to learn and then recognize a wide variety of behaviors to choose from in order to follow our genetic instructions and meet our basic needs.

BUILDING SELF-ESTEEM

As adults, we need to learn to trust and believe our children's signals as the regulators for their bodies and the effectiveness of their behavior to change the world to be as they want. We need to learn to get out of their business and allow them to learn the communication signals that their bodies send to them. Just as a baby will no longer eat after it has had enough food, we need to believe that this is true for our children when they get older. When our child tells us that he has had enough to eat, we need to trust and believe this child instead of insisting he eat three more bites. If, after taking a bite, our child tells us that he does not like a certain food, we need to believe him and not insist he eat all of this food then be rewarded with dessert. The challenge is harder when our child tells us he is no longer hungry for dinner, but when dessert arrives the child tells us he has plenty of room for more than one helping of the treat. We need to get out of our child's business of learning to hear his own signals and allow him to eat what he finds enjoyable.

If we are concerned that our child will only eat sweets, then we should have fewer sweets in our house for our child to choose from. If we want our child to eat more fruits and vegetables and less ice cream and cookies, we should make fruits and vegetables available to our child at every meal and serve ice cream and cookies only for very special occasions. If we allow our child to regulate his food intake based on the signals he gets from his own body, not based on pacifying rules and regulations made outside his body (parents' choice of eating all the main course before being allowed dessert), we will do much in helping our children learn self-confidence, build their self-esteem (liking and believing in themselves and their bodies) and avoid the potential issue of food disorders later in life. This may seem extreme. The extreme part is allowing our children to learn and trust their own body signals. After all, their bodies are going to be with them for the rest of their lives. Their parents, hopefully, are not.

The principle of asking our children to self-evaluate and then believing their self-evaluation applies not only to food, but to all other need areas in their life. Our children can learn to increase their awareness of their self-evaluation as their cognitive and logical thinking processes mature. We can rely on our children's ability to self-evaluate honestly and share this evaluation with us. If we create an environment where our children's self-evaluation is believed and honored by us, then we are creating conditions where our children can feel safe to share their self-evaluation with us. If our child shares his self-evaluation with us, and we don't believe him or we overrule him, then the chances are good that in the future our child will stop sharing his self-evaluation with us. If this trend continues, eventually our child may also stop believing and trusting his own self-evaluation.

> *Mother:* "Kevin, have you finished all of your homework?"
>
> *Kevin:* "Yep."
>
> *Mother:* "How could that be? You barely spent 30 minutes doing your work. Are you sure you did all of your assignments?"
>
> *Kevin:* "Well, I did it all. We didn't have that much homework tonight."
>
> *Mother:* "Maybe you better let me check it."

Although this mother may have the best of intentions in wanting to help her son have success in school, her job is to help her son self-evaluate his homework accomplishment. Then the mother needs to trust what her son tells her. If Kevin receives information from his teacher that he needs to improve the quality or completion of his homework effort, Kevin can once again self-evaluate whether or not doing better in school is a picture in his quality world. If it is, then Kevin can self-evaluate his level of effort as it relates to helping him have the school success that Kevin wants. The mother's job is to help her son self-evaluate but not to evaluate Kevin's behavior and performance for Kevin.

If Kevin's mother continues in the above direction, one of two things may eventually happen. The first possibility is that Kevin begins to lie or be deceitful to his mother. Kevin will eventually know that no matter what his answer, his mother won't trust him. So Kevin may begin to share a false self-evaluation with his mother. The second possibility is that Kevin will begin to doubt his own judgment, his own self-evaluations. He thinks his mother might be right. He begins to fear that he hasn't worked enough, and so even though the 30 minutes Kevin spent on school work was enough for this evening, he may begin to doubt his own ability to judge and evaluate his behavior and performance.

Although what I am suggesting may seem difficult for some parents to believe, if we create an environment where our children feel safe to self-evaluate and are trusted and believed when they share their self-evaluation with us, we will have taken giant steps in helping our children learn about the miracle and wonders of their internal self-regulating system.

Our efforts are better spent learning how to ask our children to pay attention to their self-evaluations and honoring and believing their answers (See Table 2 below.) We can spend a great deal of time asking our child what he wants, what his quality world picture is. Following this, can be time spent in asking our child to share with us all the behaviors he is presently using to get what he wants. As was mentioned in the last chapter, we can even add information about our child's behaviors based on information we have observed of what he is doing to get what he wants. Then we ask our child to self-evaluate the effectiveness of all of these behaviors in moving him in the direction to get what it is he wants. Our child's job is to pay attention to his own internal signals that will let him know whether his behaviors are effective or ineffective. Our job is to set the environment where our child can self-evaluate and then believe and honor this. Our child's job is to self-evaluate.

TABLE 2

SELF-EVALUATION
ASKING PROCESS

WHAT DO YOU WANT?

Quality World Picture

WHAT ARE YOU DOING NOW TO GET WHAT YOU WANT?

Total Behaviors Used (acting, thinking, feeling, physiology)

SELF-EVALUATION:

Is what you're doing getting you what you want?

Is what you're doing moving you in the direction you want to go?

Is what you're doing helping?

Is what you're doing against the rules?

ASK DETAILS ABOUT THE QUALITY WORLD PICTURES.
GATHER ALL BEHAVIORS, INCLUDING THOSE YOU OBSERVE.
BELIEVE AND HONOR THE SELF-EVALUATION GIVEN.

LIVING WITH CONSEQUENCES

What do we as parents do when the honest self-evaluation our child shares with us is different from what we believe or what we want to hear? Let's look at two specific examples.

🏠　　🏠　　🏠　　🏠

Vickie, mother of preschooler Janet, is planning a morning running errands with the final stop at the public library. She and Janet have followed this routine before, adding the library as their final stop from a suggestion Janet made months earlier that doing something fun at the end of their morning jobs helps Janet. As part of their usual ritual, Vickie asks Janet to visit the bathroom before they leave.

"I don't have to go." Janet tells her mother.

"Are you sure?" Vickie wants to double-check because there isn't a public restroom easily available until their final library stop.

"I just went," Janet explains. "I don't have to go again."

"Remember, once we get on the road I won't know where a public bathroom is. If you have to go, it may take us a little while to find you one." Vickie is pointing out the potential consequences of Janet's decision and letting her know what may happen.

"I know," says Janet. "I'm all ready to leave."

🏠　　🏠　　🏠　　🏠

At this point, despite what Vickie may believe or have experienced in the past, her job is to believe the self-evaluation that Janet has shared with her. Even though in less than 30 minutes, Janet may proclaim that she has to go to the bathroom, Vickie's job is to ask her daughter to tune into her own internal signals, then believe what her daughter tells her. If Janet develops a repeated pattern of telling her mother she does not need to use the bathroom before they leave the house, only to discover 15 or 20 or 30 minutes later that she does indeed need to go, then Vickie's job is to help her daughter learn to listen more carefully to her internal signals before they leave the house.

Vickie's job is not to undermine her daughter's self-evaluation by doubting or second guessing her. Vickie certainly can explain to her daughter that even though Vickie may have just used the toilet 15 minutes before they leave, Vickie makes another stop to be sure her bladder is completely empty because she does not like the feeling of being somewhere when she needs to go and having no toilet easily available. Vickie can point out how she handles this problem differently than her daughter, thus giving Janet additional information so that Janet might learn to behave differently. She has also pointed out the potential consequences of the decision Janet is making so Janet might change her self-evaluation based on the additional information. But Vickie is still allowing Janet her own self-evaluation. By allowing Janet to self-evaluate and experience her own consequences of this self-evaluation, Vickie is helping Janet rely on her own internal self-regulating system.

📖 📖 📖 📖

Sixteen-year old Martha is negotiating with her father Stan, to stay at a girlfriend's house this evening following her attendance at a school dance. There are several girls hoping to participate in this schedule of events. Stan knows the girl where Martha wants to stay, as well as the girl who will be driving the troops to the dance and then to the sleep-over. He knows all of the six girls involved with the plan. The potential difficulty is that Jill, one of the girls who is going to be part of the group, got into trouble with school and with her parents a few months ago. During a school sponsored skiing trip, Jill and the three other girls she roomed with were caught smoking pot in their room. Jill's parents made the long trip to Vermont to retrieve their daughter, who was suspended from school for two weeks. Her parents also got her immediately involved with a drug counselor. Although Stan does not believe that Jill is a bad kid, just a kid who made a bad choice, he is still worried. Martha is trying to convince her father that his concerns are ill founded.

Martha: "Dad, it's all right. None of the girls that Jill was involved with on the ski trip are going to be part of the sleep-over."

Stan: "I just don't want to put you in a situation where you may need to make a choice that may be hard to make. What if Jill meets some of these other girls at the dance and decides to smoke some more dope?"

Martha: "Dad, I don't smoke pot and I don't use drugs. None of the other girls who are going to Marcie's use drugs either. Jill knows this. If she is stupid enough to get back involved with other kids who use drugs, we won't let her come to Marcie's."

Stan: "Have you already discussed that possibility with the other girls?"

Martha: "Well, no. But I'm sure they would all agree with me that is the best plan. Come on, Dad. It's not fair for you to punish me for something that Jill did and that I had nothing to do with."

Stan couldn't disagree with his daughter. He was just concerned about doing whatever he needed to protect his daughter and help her make the best choices for herself. He decides to use Martha's self-evaluation to help him make a decision.

Stan: "Martha, do you believe that you will be able to make good choices for yourself if you go to the dance and then to Marcie's house with these girls, even if Jill is there and makes bad choices?"

Martha: "Yes, Dad, I do. First of all, no matter what choices Jill makes for herself, she doesn't rule me. Second of all, it's not as if I haven't seen Jill since she got into trouble. I see her every day in school. I really think she is making better decisions since she got into so much trouble. She hasn't been hanging around any of those kids she was with on the ski trip. But whether she does or doesn't decide to use drugs or drink, for that matter, I'm going to make the choice not to do either of those things. It's dumb! Especially on school grounds or at a school event. Talk about asking to get caught!"

Stan agrees to let his daughter go to the dance and then to her friend's house for an over-night. Although he is still worried, he has asked her to evaluate the situation for herself, including her ability to handle the potential difficulties. Although he may spend a worried night, he realizes that he must rely on his daughter's good judgment and her honest appraisal of herself and the situation.

Stan is allowing his daughter to self-evaluate and then relying on this honest self-evaluation to help him decide what to do. He pointed out the potential consequences and shared with her his fears and concerns. Despite all of that information, Martha was still confident that she could make choices that were best for her. Beyond that, all Stan could do was to have faith that the values he has taught his daughter, as well as teaching Martha to pay attention to her own self-evaluations from a very early age, would help her make good choices.

When our children make evaluations that are different from what we believe or different from what we want to hear, all that we can do is to point out the potential consequences that we foresee from their self-evaluation. If giving this additional information does not change our child's evaluation, there is nothing more that we can do. We can point out our worry and concern and our wish for them to make a different decision, but it is each person's self-evaluation that motivates a person to behave differently. As parents, we can influence our child to change his mind, including his self-evaluation, but we cannot make someone self-evaluate differently.

As long as we have created an atmosphere where our child feels safe to share his self-evaluation honestly with us because he does not fear the consequences we might impose if he tells us his truth, then we can expect that sometimes our children will self-evaluate differently from what we would wish. Hopefully, we will hold a quality world picture of an honest, open and safe relationship with our children so that hearing the truth, even when it may be unpleasant or different from what we hope, is the most important aspect of our relationship.

RULES HELP TO REGULATE

At this point, let me also say a word about rules. We will discuss this issue in greater length in Chapter 8, the chapter on discipline. However, I do not want any parent to finish this chapter thinking that it is the child's self-evaluation alone that regulates the guiding rules and regulations within a household. As we have already discussed, self-evaluation is the internal self-regulating system that allows us to know when the world we want matches the world we are experiencing, as well as letting us know when a mismatch exists. Part of a parent's job is also to establish the rules within the house that regulate the values and guiding principles for acceptable behavior within a family. These rules should be based on the general guiding principle that all members of the family can meet their needs and follow their genetic instructions without interfering with other members of the family doing the same. So even though our two-year old son may self-evaluate that hitting his younger sister is an effective behavior in helping him play with his truck without his sister's grabbing it from him, as a family we may have established a rule that hitting is not permitted. When we ask our son to evaluate the effectiveness of his behavior, we need to ask an additional self-evaluation question: Is hitting his sister following the family rule of no hitting? We may be aware that his hitting is his best behavioral attempt to get the world to be as he wants, free from his sister's interfering with his truck game. But there are additional quality world pictures, called the family rules, established to help all in the family best meet their needs. Although our child may not care about the family rule of hitting at the time he has a strong urge to hit his sister to get his truck back, we still need to ask the child to self-evaluate his behavior in relation to rules, as well as his own personal quality world desires. So be assured that when we ask our child to self-evaluate, we are asking for him to be aware of not only his own internal system, but also how he fits into and lives within the context of the whole social system.

PUTTING IT ALL TOGETHER

Now we have a complete explanation for how our brain works and how and why we behave. Let's put it all together. (See Table 3, page 78.) We are all born with genetic instructions driving our behaviors to satisfy our basic genetic needs for survival, love and belonging, power, freedom and fun. As we experience the world and get strong, pleasurable, good feelings when our needs are satisfied, we hold onto these experiences as sensory pictures in our quality world. Our quality world representations drive us to behave in the world to have the real world match the pictures in our quality world. We have an idea of what we want. We perceive the world and discover, through our self-evaluation, that what we want and what we are experiencing are different. This self-evaluation is felt as an urge to behave. We behave in the world in an attempt to change the world to be what we want. As we behave in the world we continuously self-evaluate the effectiveness of our behaviors. If our self-evaluation tells us that our behaviors are not effective in changing the world to match our quality world picture, we continue to behave. We evaluate what behaviors we could use that would be the most effective in changing the world. If our new behavior is effective, we self-evaluate that what we want and what we are experiencing are a match. This match is felt as a pleasurable, positive feeling.

TABLE 3

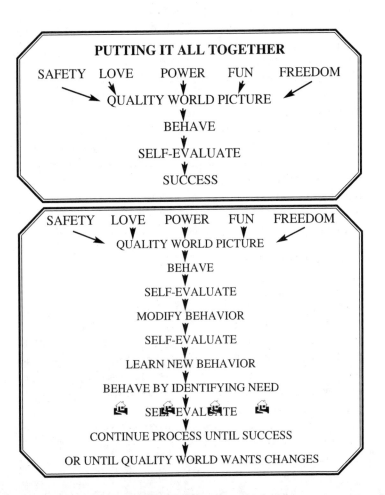

PUTTING IT ALL TOGETHER

SAFETY   LOVE   POWER   FUN   FREEDOM
→ QUALITY WORLD PICTURE ←
BEHAVE
SELF-EVALUATE
SUCCESS

SAFETY   LOVE   POWER   FUN   FREEDOM
→ QUALITY WORLD PICTURE ←
BEHAVE
SELF-EVALUATE
MODIFY BEHAVIOR
SELF-EVALUATE
LEARN NEW BEHAVIOR
BEHAVE BY IDENTIFYING NEED
SELF-EVALUATE
CONTINUE PROCESS UNTIL SUCCESS
OR UNTIL QUALITY WORLD WANTS CHANGES

Michael, 15 years old, attends drivers' education classes during summer vacation. He has put driving into his quality world as a behavior that will help him meet all of his needs: power and freedom to drive himself where he wants to go, when he wants to go; driving seems like a fun activity, playing his radio loudly, feeling the power of the engine respond as he pushes his foot on the accelerator; love and belonging because he can take his friends with him on his various excursions. He has been talking about "when my parents buy me a car" since he was 13 years old even though his mother has assured him his parents will be making no such purchase for him.

He successfully completes the classroom drivers' education, as well as the behind the wheel training. Several months after his 16th birthday, he passes his driver's test and obtains his driver's license. All along he has been self-evaluating that all that he is doing, attending classes and practicing behind the wheel, is helping him move in the direction of getting his driver's license. The day he successfully completes his driver's test and becomes a licensed driver he is full of pleasure and pride, showing off his driver's license to everyone he knows.

Several months after he has his license, Michael puts a new picture into his quality world. He wants his own car. Not only does he want to drive, but he has refined his quality world picture to include the increased freedom, power and fun he believes being in full possession of a car will bring. Driven by this new picture, Michael begins his search for a car. Although Michael's ideal quality world car is a black Porsche 911, he is willing to settle for a lesser car, one he can afford. He reads the used car want ads in the daily paper as well as the weekly circular. He discusses his options with his father and grandfather. He talks with other friends who have their own car, discovering what method they used to purchase a car successfully. All of these behaviors are purposeful, driven by his quality world picture of wanting a car as well as the self-evaluation urge to behave when he realizes that he has no car of his own in the world.

His diligent search leads to discovering a perfect used vehicle, a small truck. In the few days between reading the ad, going to look at the truck and then deciding to make an offer to the owner, someone else purchases the truck. Michael experiences a large gap between what he wants, the truck, and what he realizes reality is bringing him, the truck is no longer available for his purchase. He behaves by feeling disappointed but more determined than ever. He continues his search.

The next time he investigates a car he discovers from the classified ads, he modifies his behavior. He goes with his father, rather than arranging for two different meeting times as he had previously. He also takes a blank check with him. If this is the car for Michael, he will not hesitate. Success! The car looks good, drives well and is the right price. Although it isn't as perfect a match of what he wanted as was the truck, this car has a standard transmission, so Michael feels powerful, an in-control driver, and so cool as he drives through the streets shifting gears. He washes, waxes and volunteers to drive his friends to all their activities. What he wanted and all that he did helped him successfully purchase a car.

Throughout this process, Michael was self-evaluating his behaviors. Was he doing what he needed to do to get what he wanted? When the answer was no, he modified his behavior. His self-evaluation helped him fine tune his behaviors to lead him to his ultimate goal and success.

🏠   🏠   🏠   🏠

As the above story illustrates, our quality world pictures, put there because they are need-fulfilling, drive us to behave in the world to follow our genetic instructions and meet our needs. Behaviors enable our success. Self-evaluation enables us to modify and adjust our behaviors.

SUMMARY

• The internal process of self-evaluating is a self-regulating system that informs us when we are getting what we want, feeling comfort, as well as when we are not getting what we want, feeling discomfort.

• We experience an urge to behave when we self-evaluate that what we want, our quality world picture, and what we are getting are not the same. We feel an urge to change the world to be closer to our quality world picture.

• Self-evaluation is a process that not only urges us to behave to increase our chances of survival, it is also a process that helps us learn increasingly complicated behaviors to help us follow our genetic instructions and meet our needs.

• Self-evaluation is a continuous process. Self-evaluations drive us to behave.

• When we feel an urge to behave, we can slow down and think before we immediately follow the urge to behave. Slowing down to become aware of the urge to behave allows us more time to evaluate which behavior may be the most effective in helping us get what we want.

• We experience pleasure and satisfaction when we self-evaluate that what we want is what we are getting. These feelings are not as strong as the feelings accompanying the self-evaluation of a mismatch between what we want and what we perceive we are getting. There is no urge to behave that accompanies the self-evaluation of a match, so the feeling may not be very strong.

• Paying attention to these matches, even though the feeling may not be strong, enables us to increase our joy and satisfaction in our lives. as well as learn the effective behaviors that help us get what we want.

• Building our child's self-esteem means asking our child to self-evaluate, then honoring and believing his self-evaluation. Our child will honestly self-evaluate and share this with us if he believes there are no negative consequences that we will impose on him for doing so.

• If our child's self-evaluation differs from our evaluation for him, we can attempt to influence him by pointing out potential consequences that our child may not be aware of. If he doesn't change his self-evaluation, we can't make him change. Instead, we must let him learn through his own experience what consequences result from his self-evaluation.

- Allowing our child to live with the consequences of his self-evaluation produces more information for his subsequent self-evaluation. These consequences may, in turn, alter our child's self-evaluation.

- Rules of the home, as well as quality world pictures, are the benchmarks against which we self-evaluate and ask our children to self-evaluate.

Chapter Five
Creating a Peaceful Place for Exploration and Discovery

A NEW PLACE

Imagine we are walking into an unfamiliar room filled with all sorts of things new to us. There are many textures to be felt, sounds to be heard and made, food and other objects awaiting our exploration through smell and taste. When we first enter this room we are exhilarated and almost overwhelmed by the unfamiliarity of it all. The longer we stand gazing at what is before us, the more we realize there is to discover.

Now imagine there is a person with us. This person is the guardian of the room. Smiling warmly, this person sweeps her hand around, inviting us to explore all there is to discover. She tells us that she will answer any questions we have. She assures us that we are safe and that all the things in the room are free from harm. "We have limitless time to discover and explore all that's here," she tells us.

Sound intriguing? Perhaps it is reminiscent of a recent vacation to a new location. Only this time we don't have to do any of the planning, nor do we have to pay! All we need to do is enjoy the limitless exploration and boundless discoveries, with a guardian present to ensure our safety and the safety of all objects in the room.

With some slight changes, we have glimpsed what the world was like for us as infants. Everything was new, including our own evolving abilities to discover and explore. The job of the parent is to be the guardian to keep the infant safe. As we have already discussed, curiosity to discover and explore is an instruction built into every human being. The guardian doesn't need to coax the infant to explore beyond providing the assurance that the baby is safe from harm. Children are born with the instruction to explore and discover the world as well as their place and abilities within the world. We do not need to urge or push this natural curiosity onto children.

GUARDIANS OF SAFETY

The job of parents as guardians is first to meet the built-in need all babies have to feel safe, secure in their knowledge that they will survive. Initially this means having all biological needs attended to: fresh air to breath freely, the temperature not too hot nor too cold, the comfort of a full tummy, and the warmth of human touch sometimes, or the freedom to wave arms and legs about sometimes. This feeling of security eventually changes to include the loving companionship of other people. The first connection desired is with the care-giver. Eventually the baby discovers that connecting with other humans is also very satisfying.

When the baby is feeling safe, she will explore all that is around her in this strange and intriguing new place. The desire to explore through all the infant's senses is a strong instruction indeed. Everything within grasp, within sight and ear-shot is beckoning the child.

Watch a curious twelve-month old as she is placed in the family room, surrounded by her familiar toys, as well as a new array of refreshments you have placed on the coffee table for company. She will naturally be pulled to explore the new things in the room: the glasses filled with iced tea, the sharp knife placed on the cheese board, as well as the crackers carefully arranged in a basket.

Not everything in the world is safe for our child. So our job is to act as protector and guardian for our child. This guardianship may extend beyond our child as well. We may have possessions in our home that are precious to us. Another aspect of our job is to guard those things we want protected from our child's exploring grasp. Some parents create a baby-proof home. That is, they put all things that they do not want their child to handle out of the child's reach. There are inexpensive outlet covers available at hardware stores to protect curious fingers from poking into high voltage places. I am not stating that all homes must be baby-proofed, but this is an option. My own personal bias was to child-proof our home, giving me a greater amount of freedom while we were home together. My husband and I placed our most valuable and most potentially dangerous possessions out of the family room, where we spent most of our time.

When we visit other households with our child, there certainly is no assurance that others will have protected our child or their possessions from harm. That is our job, as the parent. I was acutely aware, when visiting my parents' home as well as my in-laws' home, how many valuable items they all kept within easy grasp of curious hands and mouths. Again, my job was to allow my children to follow their natural instruction to explore all there was to discover, while ensuring safety for all humans, possessions and family pets.

Watching our children follow their genetic instruction to satisfy their curiosity when they are very young is easy to see. This same instruction continues throughout our child's life, as well as our own lives. Children are curious and want to explore, no matter what the age. Our job as the guardians for our children's safety never stops but changes as our children grow and mature. Instead of being our child's constant companion, ever present and vigilant to potential hazards and dangers, we teach our children how to be alert for these dangers and hazards themselves. Being our child's guardian of safety includes educating our child, arming her with knowledge and information.

A child is curious about her own body as well. A baby's attention can remain focused on her own hand as she moves it to her mouth, away from her mouth, to her mouth, etc. This same exploration includes a seven-year old discovering the fascinating sounds she can make with her mouth, with her fingers and with various combinations of body parts.

Not only can our bodies entertain us with various and curious sounds, but new and pleasurable sensations can be found in our own body. Children discover their own sexuality and sexual feelings as they explore their bodies.

When our child matures and reaches puberty, biological changes begin to transform the sensations our child will discover in her body. Our child will continue to be curious, wanting to understand and explore. By providing our child with information about the changes that she is experiencing, we participate and support her exploration. As she grows and continues to mature, she will become aware of the changes and differences in close relationships. Suddenly she is aware of her sexual feelings toward another person. Although pleasurable, these new sensations may be confusing. She is curious and may want to explore these feelings and sensations. Our job continues to be teacher, educating and informing our child. Armed with knowledge and information, our child can be aware of the potential hazards and dangers, as well as pleasures that are part of her sexuality.

LEARNING NEW BEHAVIORS

A child will use a wide variety of familiar and effective behaviors to explore her ever widening world. The strong urge to discover even more will also lead our child to develop brand new behaviors to assist her in this exploration.

When my son Paul was about eight months old, he lay on his back on a blanket in the middle of our living room floor. I watched his eyes focus on the shiny brass magazine rack across the room from him. Paul used all of his familiar, organized behaviors that he had learned up to this point. He began sucking, salivating and smacking his lips and mouth. He flailed his arms about, kicking and rocking to and fro, up and down. All the time his eyes remained focused on the shiny inviting object. He tried whimpering as well. Frustrated because none of these behaviors was helping him get any closer to being able to put the shiny brass in his mouth for exploration, he tried something new. He rocked himself enough to roll over onto his belly. The magazine rack was still within sight as he lay on his stomach, raised head supported by his bent elbows. I watched with great delight as my son learned how to creep for the first time.

Without apparent hesitation he crept his way over to the magazine rack, grabbing hold of the side and sucking with all his might on the upper part that was most easily within his range.

      🖕   🖕   🖕   🖕

This child's strong desire to explore something newly discovered within his environment helped him to develop a brand new set of effective behaviors spontaneously to satisfy his strong curiosity urge. Although I was quick to call family relatives to brag proudly about the new developmental milestone that Paul had accomplished, Paul was much more impressed by the texture and taste of the shiny brass than he was at his ability to creep. Creeping, for him, was only a means to an end. As his mother, I was delighted that he had successfully accomplished a complicated series of behaviors that would eventually lead to his ability to walk. He was less impressed by these new behaviors, except he now had more behaviors to help him explore and discover more of this new world where he found himself. Because these new behaviors had been effective in helping him get what he wanted, he remembered them and used them again, furthering his memory of them as effective behaviors to be tried again when he was faced with other experiences where he wanted something that he was not getting.

This pattern, using familiar, effective behaviors when we are faced with something we want that we are not getting, continues from infancy until death. In addition, we create new behaviors through trial and error when the familiar, effective behaviors are not working in a new situation. As we get older, the number of effective behaviors available to us increases. When all of our familiar and previously effective behaviors do not work to help us get what we want, then we will create new behaviors and try them if the desire to get what we want is strong enough.

Included in the behaviors we learn is the behavior of giving up. At some point in our life, we learn that giving up is an effective behavior. When we are faced with the frustration of not getting what we want, we may ultimately give up, rather than creating new behaviors that may or may not work.

Although initially this may seem to be less than a desirable behavior, giving up may be vital for our very survival. Continuing to pursue something that is very likely unreachable could lead to a person's exhaustion and death if he did not decide to give up the pursuit. After spending time around a young child who persists in attempting to get what she wants, you may also be familiar with our own child's opposite, but equally effective behavior of persevering. Driven to get what she wants, she may persevere, continuing to create new behaviors, rather than giving up!

LOVE, POWER, FUN AND FREEDOM

Our child is born with the drive to follow all her genetic instructions from birth and throughout her life. The drive to belong and experience loving relationships, the drive to feel recognized and powerful, the drive to discover and explore her environment through play, the drive to be free to move within her environment so she can discover new things in her world, are all present at birth. Our job, as the parent and guardian, is to provide opportunities for our child to satisfy these genetic instructions and drives. Our job is not to meet these needs for our child because we can't.

For example, when our child lets us know she is hungry, we can provide her with food. In order for her to feel satiated, she must eat by herself. Obviously, our eating a peanut butter and jelly sandwich when our child is hungry will not help her become less hungry. So too, when our child lets us know she wants more freedom, we must provide this opportunity for her. We may take our baby out of her playpen and allow her to explore her bedroom under our supervision. We may allow our seven-year old the freedom of an overnight stay at a friend's house. We may allow our teenager to attend a high school basketball game with friends. Our job, as the parent and guardian, is to provide a safe and secure opportunity for our child to follow her basic genetic instruction to be free, just as it is our job to provide the opportunity for our child to eat. Our job is to provide an environment where all the child's instructions can be followed so she can satisfy all her needs effectively.

PEACEFUL PLACE FOR ALL

Creating a peaceful place in which our child can grow and flourish means we must remember the instructions our child is born attempting to follow. Every member of the household is also driven by these same instructions. The job of the adults, the parents and the guardians, is to provide an environment where all family members can meet their needs for safety and survival, love and belonging, power, fun and freedom. This is the key to peaceful parenting. This is the key to a peaceful household.

The child is not the only person in the household who is attempting to follow these instructions. Every member of the family is also attempting to follow these instructions and meet these needs. As the adult in the household, it is a parent's job to provide an environment with a wide variety of opportunities for need-satisfaction, so that all members will be able to meet their needs. The opportunities for satisfying the drive for freedom for a three-year old should be different than those for an eleven-year old, for example. In addition, if we continually introduce new opportunities for need-satisfaction to our children by allowing them to interact with an ever widening world, we are also increasing the opportunities for need-satisfaction.

DIFFERENT QUALITY WORLDS

As we have already discussed, even though all people are born with the same genetic instructions, we do not all share the same quality world pictures of what is need-satisfying. Creating an environment where family members can meet their basic needs means accommodating the various quality world pictures that each member of the family has of what will be need-satisfying. Creating a need-satisfying environment, then becomes increasingly challenging. Providing an environment with a wide variety of opportunities, rather than only one or two alternatives, helps in meeting this challenge. Let's use food to help explain this concept.

Everyone in the family will become hungry. This is part of the biological drive based on the need to survive. But not everyone in the family agrees on what is the best food to satisfy hunger. A toddler might think chicken fingers would be really tasty. A teenager enthusiastically endorses pizza. The adult might want a baked potato with steamed vegetables, including brussel sprouts. All members of the household are driven by their genetic need to survive, but their ideas of what will satisfy their hunger are vastly different.

These varying quality world pictures develop through previous experiences. Each person ate one of the above foods and experienced pleasure and satiation. However, tomorrow when we ask our toddler or our teenager what they are hungry for, the answers may change. We have many pictures in our quality world of what is need-satisfying. Even when we choose food to eat, we are following more than just the instruction to survive. If we feel safe and secure, knowing that we will survive and have the freedom to choose a wide variety of foods that are tasty, we will make varying choices. As we just talked about, part of the job of parenting is to introduce our child to a wide variety of tastes and food textures, helping her to follow her instruction to explore more and more of her world, including various foods that are delicious as well as nutritious.

Luckily, often what happens in families is that the taste for foods is very similar. The child develops pictures in her quality world of food that is tasty based on her experiences of foods. Her experiences come from the foods she is fed by her parent. Parents often feed their child food that parents enjoy. So usually a mother who is not a fan of liver will not introduce liver into her toddler's diet. A mother who loves artichokes may introduce this food to her child and discover that her child enjoys this food as much as she. As a parent we have the opportunity to influence our child's tastebud development.

We develop the pictures in our quality world based on our need-satisfying experiences. We hold onto the memory of something when it is need-satisfying. This becomes something that we want. Parents have the ability to influence the pictures that satisfy their children's basic genetic instructions because they are the people who introduce much of the world to their children. In our child's early life, much of her environment and world are influenced by us. Each time we offer our child one food or another, we are introducing her to another possibility for need-satisfaction. With her enjoyment of this food, our child places this food into her quality world of a need-satisfying food she will want again.

But influence does not mean dictate. As an enthusiastic lobster eater, I was not able to convince successfully one of my sons that lobster tasted good. Even though both my husband and I have a strong and specific picture in our quality worlds of a lobster meal being among our favorite dining pleasures, my son is not convinced. He would rather have hot dogs.

The same principle carries over for the other basic needs as well. All family members have a different picture in their quality world of what is included in a perfect family vacation (a time when we are driven to meet all of our needs, especially the needs for love, fun and freedom). Certainly my husband and I have influenced our children. We spend many family vacations hiking and biking in the New England mountains. Our children agree that this is a fun vacation. They put this picture into their quality worlds based on previous family vacations in the New England mountains, where they met their needs enjoying hikes and bike rides. Their favorite family vacation, however, is spending a week at Disney World, where no bikes are ridden nor trails hiked. We provided this opportunity once for the family, and the boys developed a strong quality world picture of Disney World as their ideal vacation.

It is through our experiences we are able to meet our needs, feeling the pleasure and joy that accompany need-satisfaction. Because much of a family's experiences are shared experiences and hopefully these experiences are also need fulfilling, families develop quality world pictures that are very similar to one another.

Certainly, quality world pictures change over time. As a child, my family vacations were camping adventures. Camping was need-fulfilling and pleasurable. It was the only experience I had of family vacations. (My parents were unable to afford any other variety or opportunity for family vacations.) However, I do not still hold this picture as an ideal vacation. Now that I am older and have had additional experiences in the world, I have changed my idea of what I find need-fulfilling and enjoyable during a family vacation. For me, a perfect vacation does not involve all the work it takes to camp. However, I still maintain a part of my childhood quality world picture. Spending time in the mountains with my family is still a need-fulfilling part of my quality world picture. I have passed this down to my own children but they may change when they get older because they will continue to experience the world with different varieties of people, places and activities. Who knows what each will have as an ideal family vacation when they are adults?

PROVIDE A VARIETY OF EXPERIENCES

Creating a peaceful place for exploration and discovery means providing an environment at home where family members are able to follow their genetic instructions and meet their needs. It also means providing an environment with enough variety that everyone can be satisfied. In addition, we continue to introduce new opportunities and aspects of the world to our children, so they can continue to discover and explore an ever widening world where needs can be met. Although this may sound like a daunting task, it is something we are already doing in our home. Whether we were aware of it or not, we were born with the genetic instructions to meet our needs for survival, love, power, fun and freedom. As we followed our genetic instructions, we created a home where we were able to follow these instructions and meet our needs.

Let us take a few moments to reflect on what is already happening in our homes. There are several people that we and our family feel connected with, including each other. Do we eat at least one meal together as a family on a regular basis? If we do, there is a sense of belonging and connectedness we all feel when we sit and eat together, especially if this can happen at least once a day.

Not only are we providing an opportunity for everyone to meet her need for love and belonging when we eat a meal together, we take this opportunity to talk with each other, listening to the important highlights of each other's day when away from each other. When we talk and listen to one another, an opportunity for meeting our need for power exists.

Who planned the meal? Does everyone have an opportunity to select some of the weekly menu? Giving each member of the family a chance to select the items on the family meal is another opportunity to meet the need for power and also the need for freedom.

Who cooked the meal? Have we allowed our child to become a cook's helper? Again, this is another opportunity for power satisfaction, as well as the opportunity for fun! (Although I must confess that I do not have a picture of cooking as a fun picture.) My children include baking cookies as a picture in their quality world. In our home they have the reputation for being the best cookie bakers, but they also want the freedom and power to say tonight is a cookie baking night, or it is not. Again, this is another opportunity for need satisfaction around food planning, preparation and eating.

NEEDS ASSESSMENT

One way we might begin to increase our own awareness of basic needs within the family is to ask each member of the household to make a list of each of his or her needs and then list the people, places, activities and things each person includes in her quality world to meet each need. (See Table 4 page 94 for an example of a single parent household, with Mom, two children and Grandmother living in the home.) Another way to approach this idea is to ask all members of the family to list all that they do during a typical weekday and a typical weekend day. Next to each item, include what genetic instruction she is following by completing each task and activity. Certainly, one item might include more than one genetic instruction. (Playing tennis helps me meet my needs for belonging, power, fun and freedom, for instance.)

Not only can we engage each family member in an activity where together you are exploring the basic needs, but we can begin to ask our child questions regularly, exploring her needs. When she comes home from school, we might ask her where she felt important while she was at school. When she comes inside after playing with friends, we might ask her what the fun things were that she played. During dinner, a regular question to all in the family might be something that they learned during the day or some new discovery made during their day. We need to ask our child which instruction she feels she is following when she completes a task and listen to words our child uses to describe events in her life. We may be amazed and how often our child spontaneously tells us, "This is fun!" or "I hate this. I have no choices," or other descriptive words that are reflective of the basic genetic needs.

TABLE 4

NEEDS ASSESSMENT

	SAFETY	LOVE	POWER	FUN	FREEDOM
Mom (33 years old)	Diet choices Aerobics classes Yearly doctor's check-up Seat belt wearer	Children Mother 3 Best girl friends Dating, no one special Siblings Co-workers	Career Being a mom Head of household Friends	Time with children Family gatherings Tennis Reading Cooking Piano playing Story time	AM meditation Aerobics class Dinner with friends Chores with children Evening with mother

	SAFETY	LOVE	POWER	FUN	FREEDOM
Hannah (8 years old)	Personal hygiene Seat belt wearer School bus safety Bicycle safety	Mom, Grandma Dad brother Alex Molly (best friend) Nana, Gramps Aunts, Uncles Cousins Teacher Some class-mates Ballet teacher	Reading Jumping rope Paper dolls Coloring Spelling Cook's helper Ballet Chore	Jumping rope Bike riding Friends over Story time Paper dolls Coloring Library visits	Jumping rope Bike riding Friends over Story time Paper dolls Coloring Library visits

	SAFETY	LOVE	POWER	FUN	FREEDOM
Alex (4 years old)	Brushes teeth Drinks millk Seat belt wearer Bike helmet Plays in yard Listens to Mom and Grandma	Mom, Grandma Dad, Hannah Nana, Grandpa Aunts, Uncles Cousins Stevie & Katie	Piano lessons Playing tag Ball catching Baker's helper Computer game	Computer games Playing ball Playing with Stevie & Katie Story time Library visits Helping Grandma bake	Choosing chore Choosing story Library visits Menu planning

	SAFETY	LOVE	POWER	FUN	FREEDOM
Grandma (69 years old)	Daily walks Healthy diet Seat belt wearer Check-ups	Children Grandchildren Bridge Club Dancing partner	Baking Bridge Artwork	Story time Family dinners Dancing Artwork	Dinners out Alex at playground Walking

FAMILY MEETINGS

A family meeting is an activity that provides an opportunity for all in the family to meet their needs. It is also a vehicle for continually evaluating how we are functioning as a family, not only in terms of providing an environment where all can follow their genetic instructions, but also in the most important and difficult job of maintaining and fostering loving relationships. This meeting can also enhance family communication. Finally, it can provide an opportunity for all members of the family to practice critical thinking.

There are at least three different kinds of meetings. The first, and the kind we should practice most frequently, is called an open-ended meeting. During the meeting, there may be some general agenda items related to the planning and functioning of the family (more on this later). But the main focus of the meeting is on facilitating discussion and sharing ideas. The purpose of this kind of meeting is to help everyone with critical thinking skills, as well as to increase experience participating in a conversation or a discussion. Each meeting should have only one topic or theme. In general, the topic should be fun, again to facilitate everyone's active participation. Following a format, where the first kinds of questions asked are defining kinds of questions, next a series of personalized questions, and finally asking some challenging questions, helps to facilitate the conversation. It is important to follow a rule of "no right or wrong answers" to any of the questions, so everyone feels safe to participate.

EXAMPLE:
Define:
What is a friend?
If Martians landed tomorrow and asked you what an Earthling means when she talks about her friends, how would you explain this to a Martian?
Personalize:
Who is your best friend? Why?
Who would you like to have as a friend that you are not friends with now? Why?
Who do you think wants to be friends with you, but you not with them? Why?

Challenge:

If your best friend told you she was going to rob a local pharmacy to steal a life-saving drug to save her mother's life because the family cannot afford it, what would you do?

A new kid comes to your school. No one likes her or tries to make friends with her because she is physically different. What would you do? What would you do if you were that kid?

As I hope you can see from the above examples, there are no right or wrong answers to these questions. Rather, our goal is to ask all to get involved by thinking and then communicating their thoughts with one another. Those who have ever had this kind of conversational experience, although perhaps not at a family meeting, already know how satisfying and much fun it can be. (See Table 5, page 98.)

The second kind of family meeting is a planning or problem solving meeting. These meetings should focus on social planning or problems that all in the family are affected by. This might be the time we plan what next summer's family vacation will be, including the budget needed and how we will all meet that budget. We might also plan a special, once-in-a-lifetime vacation because we need more than a few months, perhaps years, to plan and budget successfully for the trip. A discussion of family chores, negotiating each person's task or chore that contributes to the smooth functioning of the household, might also be an agenda item for one meeting. Any issue that is a problem for the whole family can be discussed at a family meeting. We would still follow the same kind of format, beginning with defining the issue, so everyone is talking about the same issue or problem. Personalized questions include each person's contribution to the problem and solution. Challenge questions focus on arriving at an agreed idea of what things would be like if the problem is solved, brainstorming all possible solutions, and finally agreeing to a final plan.

EXAMPLE:

Define:

Problem: Kitchen table is the family's "dumping ground"

Does everyone understand the problem?

Personalize:

What is each person presently doing to contribute to the problem? (Each person answers for herself only.)

Does everyone have some other place to put the items they are presently putting on the kitchen table?

Challenge:

If the problem were solved, what would the kitchen table look like?

How do we want things to look if things were better?

What are all the ideas we can think of that would solve the problem?

Of all of these ideas, what is each person willing to do to contribute to the solution?

What is our final plan? When will we review our plan?

I would discourage dealing with an individual child's behavioral problems at a family meeting. Those kinds of problems should be dealt with on an individual basis. Our child deserves the privacy of discussing her personal business on an individual basis. In addition, she may also be needing extra special attention from her parent that cannot be provided at a family meeting. This issue will be discussed more fully in Chapter 8, "Peaceful Disciplining," and Chapter 9, "Behavior Is Not The Problem."

There are family meetings where family rules are discussed, created and modified. For more information about this kind of meeting, refer to Chapter 8, "Peaceful Disciplining."

Holding family meetings once a week or once every other week helps to maintain the momentum and interest in the meetings. All family members should be expected to attend. Rotating who facilitates the meetings also allows everyone to share the power, with younger children aided by a parent. Rules for the meeting should be established. A problem solving meeting can be used to establish these rules. Each meeting should begin with a review of the rules. Any person who is visiting the family when a family meeting is scheduled should be invited to attend and participate. Having a bowl, tin, box or some other kind of container, where all can contribute ideas for agenda items at a meeting, also helps meet needs for freedom and power.

In addition, each meeting can conclude with a discussion of the weekly menu, family schedule of various activities or events anticipated in the following week, as well as setting the television schedule for the week. Although these items are not necessary, they are frequently issues that affect everyone in the family, every week. Including them on the meeting agenda can help all participate and be informed of what is occurring for the family in the week ahead.

TABLE 5

FAMILY MEETINGS

PURPOSE: Need fulfilling opportunity to enhance critical thinking and enhance family communication

KINDS: Open-ended
Planning
Problem solving rules

WHEN: Once a week

WHO: All family members

INCLUDE: Menu planning
Activity schedule
Television schedule

OPEN-ENDED MEETING

"THE LOTTERY"

If our family won $11 million in the lottery, how would each of us want to spend the money?

If we each had a portion of the money, just for ourself, what would we do with it?

If we had more money than we could ever need for all of our lifetimes and still had money left over, what do you think we should do?

What good could come from winning the lottery?

What bad might come from winning?

Should we budget any of our money for entering lotteries?

These are general guidelines and suggestions for a family meeting. I hope that each family will create and modify a family meeting so it best meets the needs of that family. I recently heard about a family who includes "Gratitude Time" during their family meeting. Sometime during the meeting, each person is asked to share something for which they are grateful, that occurred the previous week. Then each person either writes this down or draws a picture of what he or she is grateful for. These papers are then displayed for all to see on the refrigerator and then finally included in the "Family Gratitude Journal" (a book similar to a family photo album).

LOOK TO THE NEEDS

Observing people's behavior and moods can also be helpful in assessing need satisfaction within your home. When people are able to follow their genetic instructions and meet their needs, they are content, happy and satisfied. Misery and upset indicate that a child is not able to meet her needs satisfactorily. Sometimes focusing on helping our child learn more effective behaviors can help. In addition, we can teach our child that she may not always be able to get what she wants (her quality world picture), but she can still get what she needs. If we continue to provide a variety of need-satisfying opportunities for our child, we may discover that ineffective behaviors are not our child's problem, rather it is her inability to follow her genetic instruction and meet a need.

A specific example through story may help clarify this point.

🏠　　🏠　　🏠　　🏠

Single mother Rachael and only child Melissa, age 6 have been engaged in a repetitive dance of uncooperativeness every weekday morning. As Rachael describes their situation, "We began to have shouting matches, escalating to the point of interfering with our enjoyment of each other's company at other times as well." In the morning, Rachael would ask Melissa to get ready for school, by asking her repeatedly to go into her room and get dressed. Melissa would continue to play with her dolls and ignore her mother's requests. Eventually Rachael's patience would run out, as well as her acute awareness of time running out, so that she would begin yelling at Melissa to get dressed. This was met with Melissa's yelling back that she would not get dressed because she was playing. Eventually Rachael would threaten Melissa with the loss of some privilege if she did not follow her mother's direction immediately. Melissa would finally comply, but with great anger, tears and upset. Rachael's upset was also apparent. This was their beginning of every day, starting with upset and anger towards one another.

Rachael began to think about working differently with Melissa. She was beginning to suspect that Melissa's upsetting and uncooperative behaviors were purposeful. Perhaps Melissa was attempting to get something she wanted, and these were the behaviors she was using. The next weekday morning, when Rachael made her request of Melissa and Melissa ignored her, Rachael introduced a new dance step. She called Melissa into her room. "What is it you want by demanding to get your way?" she asked Melissa. "I want to go first," is what Melissa answered. She explained further to her mother that she was always required to do what her mother wanted first and was never able to do what she wanted first. Rachael, buoyed by the difference this morning's interaction was taking, took another step toward her daughter by asking, "If I let you do what you want to first, then you will listen to me when I ask you to do something?" Melissa nodded her head, then told her mother that she wanted to start going to the park again with her mother.

As upsetting as this information was to Rachael because she realized her daughter was feeling neglected by her, it was profoundly helpful. When she wasn't working or going to college, Rachael spent all of her time with Melissa. She also began to realize that the time they spent together was not doing things together, rather they were in the house together, each engaged in her own individual activity. Melissa wasn't feeling loved and connected to her mother simply by proximity.

Rachael began that very day by making a date with Melissa to go to the park together. They began to spend more time playing and doing things that Melissa re-

quested and that they both enjoyed. Included in this change is also their morning routine. When there is still more than enough time for each to get ready to begin the day, Rachael asks Melissa what she would like to do first, before she needs to get dressed and ready for school. Melissa is full of ideas. Sometimes they read a story together. Sometimes they sing a few songs to- gether. Sometimes they hug and tickle one another. Following this time together, that is directed by Melissa's desire to go first, Rachael directs the timing to get ready for the day. Melissa cooperatively and unhesi- tatingly dresses and packs her backpack filled with her school papers and lunch box. Rachael doesn't need to ask more than once.

🏠   🏠   🏠   🏠

Melissa was doing the best she knew in meeting her need for love and belonging with her mother. She was refusing to cooperate and arguing with her mother, not very effective be- haviors, but the most effective available to her. Rachael could have spent time with Melissa, helping her learn more effective behaviors. Because she took the time to listen to what it was that Melissa wanted, she realized that she needed to provide more effective opportunities for Melissa to meet her needs. Instead of focusing directly on Melissa's behaviors, Rachael helped create more opportunities for Melissa to meet her needs.

Although Melissa said that she wanted to go first, this may not have been possible every morning. As Rachael and Melissa worked together, Melissa was able to get more of what she needed. She still wanted to go first and had several, very specific quality world pictures of what that meant. If she was able to get more of what she needed, she was able to tolerate those times when she could not get what she wanted. Together, Rachael and Melissa were able to provide a wide variety of al- ternative ways they could get more of what they both needed: loving and connecting with one another.

SUMMARY

- Babies are born with the drive to explore and discover all the wonders of the world, of their own bodies, and of their own abilities and capabilities.

- Parents are the guardians for our children as they explore. Our job is to provide an environment that is safe for them and from them, so children can follow their inherent curiosity.
- As children are driven to explore and discover, they will learn new behaviors to help in their explorations.
- We are also the guardians of our children's other needs. That is, we need to provide an environment where our children are safe and can follow their instruction to be loving, powerful, playful and free.
- Creating an environment where everyone in our family has a variety of opportunities to meet basic needs is a parent's job.
- Although all family members have the same genetic instructions, each of us has different quality world pictures of what is need-satisfying. Thus, providing an atmosphere with a variety of opportunities to satisfy needs helps with the wide variety of quality world pictures that each member of the family feels is need-satisfying.
- Experiences that are need-satisfying feel good and become the pictures in our quality world of what we want in the world. Because parents introduce people, places, activities and experiences to their child, they influence their child's quality world pictures.
- Through specific activities described in this chapter or through continual discussions, parents can assess their own need-satisfaction, as well as that of other family members. This information can be used to enhance or improve the opportunities provided for the family to follow genetic instructions and meet needs.
- Family meetings can provide another opportunity for need-satisfaction and enhance family relationships and communication, as well as facilitate critical thinking.
- General attitudes of contentment, happiness and satisfaction indicate an environment where people are able to meet their needs. General attitudes of misery, upset and unhappiness indicate that more variety and opportunities for need-satisfaction need to be included in the family environment.

Chapter Six
Ages and Stages

BIOLOGY

From birth until death, human behavior is an attempt to satisfy our biological and psychological needs. The psychological needs evolved from our biological need to survive. Just as we are born with an urge to behave when we are thirsty (a biological need), so too, we are aware of an urge to behave when we enter a room filled with people. Upon entering a room, we begin searching for someone we know. Seeking a familiar person to connect with is our urge to behave to satisfy the genetic instruction for love and belonging (a psychological need).

Driven to behave to follow our genetic instructions increases the possibility that we will learn behaviors enabling us to function as independent adults, no longer dependent on our parents for our survival. Although there are other animals that are not dependent on their parents because they are born instinctively knowing all the behaviors necessary to ensure their survival (turtles, for example), this is not true for humans. During childhood, we are dependent on our parents (or some other adult). Initially parents provide for our us. As we grow, we are driven to learn how to provide for ourselves. Maintaining a close relationship with our care-giver, our provider and teacher, ensures we will live. This also assures that we will learn all we need to know to continue to live. Biologically, the parent-child bond secures that children will grow to sexual maturity, to then produce more children, guaranteeing the survival of the human species.

Children need to cooperate with their care-giver in order to be certain that their care-giver will remain involved, tending to them while they are still too young to care for themselves. Children also need to develop the ability to compete so that they will have the necessary behaviors to survive in the world on their own without their care-giver. Thus, the two categories of learning that are vital for a child's survival are the ability to cooperate and the ability to compete.

COMPLEMENTARY

Although initially it may appear as if these two aspects are opposites, it is useful to conceptualize them as two complementary halves that complete a whole. Opposites imply learning either cooperative behaviors or competitive behaviors, but both are necessary for the ultimate independence of adulthood. Learning effective cooperative and competitive behaviors means a person will learn all the necessary behaviors for independent life. Although cooperative behaviors contrast with competitive behaviors, both mutually support the ultimate goal of independence. Each half supplies what the other half lacks.

It is necessary for a child to learn the complementary behaviors of cooperation and competition for independence, the ultimate goal of childhood. Genetic instructions drive a child to behave and learn new behaviors. We can conceptualize our genetic instructions, our psychological needs, as the whole circle of needs. This whole is divided into two complementary halves of cooperative and competitive needs, with the need for survival remaining the central axis around which the other needs evolve.

The need for love and belonging, as well as the need for fun are the cooperative needs. That is, we must learn and use effective cooperative behaviors to meet the need for love and belonging and the need for fun successfully.

The need for power and the need for freedom are the competitive needs. That is, we learn and use effective competitive behaviors in order to meet these needs effectively and successfully. The whole circle of our psychological needs can be divided into two complementary halves: love and fun are the cooperative half, power and freedom are the competitive half.

LOVE AND FUN - THE COOPERATIVE NEEDS

In order to love and be loved by others, a child must be willing to cooperate with another, so that each can get to know the other without conflict or challenges. From personal experience I hope we all can readily recognize that being in a loving relationship feels cooperative. Sometimes we become willing to do something that we don't want to do because it means we will be with our child. Luckily, our child also reciprocates. Sometimes I attend a baseball game with my children, and sometimes my children visit an art gallery with me. Even though for me, watching baseball, or for my children, visiting an art gallery, isn't necessarily among our favorite activities, we are each willing to cooperate with the other. In so doing, we spend time with each other, get to better know one another, love and belong with each other. The activity is not so important. Spending time together, enjoying one another while building creative positive shared memories with one another is what helps us develop and maintain a loving relationship with each other.

Fun frequently involves activities with other people. In order for members of a soccer team to compete together successfully, they must learn to function cooperatively as a team, for example. Behaving playfully with another person usually means knowing him well enough to know what he would consider to be playful. Teasing, for some, is fun and playful, but others find it hurtful. Sitting around a camp fire singing songs is a cooperative, fun activity for some.

POWER AND FREEDOM - THE COMPETITIVE NEEDS

Running for a political office involves competitive and powerful behaviors. Not only does the candidate want to win the race, but this necessitates beating the other candidate at the voting polls. A teacher wants to behave powerfully in the classroom, to be able to influence the learning activities of the students. Teachers want to convince their students that learning what the teacher is asking will add quality to the students' lives. This involves influencing behaviors, including competing with the other interests and distractions in the students' lives.

Each of us wants to be part of a group, feel as if we belong and are accepted in a group (cooperation). But each of us also wants to be recognized as a special individual within the group, recognized as a distinct person whose presence and contributions in the group improve the quality of the group. A child wants to be part of his soccer team, feeling as if he belongs. He also wants to hear how much the team missed him during his absence due to an illness. This desire for power and recognition within a group means people will behave competitively.

Freedom can also be viewed using a competitive perspective. The history of the United States is a clear example. Freedom of religion meant that people fought and died for the right to choose another way to worship their God, different from the mandated state religion. Freedom of speech means that people can express their own opinion, even when that opinion may not be sanctioned by the prevailing culture. Representation for taxation or the ability to have our voice heard and represented within the government because we are tax-paying citizens, was the freedom demanded by American revolutionary colonists. For our forefathers and foremothers, freedom to be the person they wanted to be, even if it was different from what the state or prevailing culture expected, was such a strong desire that the country behaved in the ultimate form of competition, war, to obtain this freedom.

AGES AND STAGES

Although we are all born with all genetic instructions from birth, there are fluctuating periods during childhood where either the cooperative or the competitive needs seem to dominate a child's behavior. These are the ages and stages of a child's life.

From birth until approximately eight months, survival is the need and instruction predominantly driving the infant's behaviors. The biological need to survive, with the accompanying psychological feeling of safety, is the dominant axis in life. When a child feels safe, he is then able to follow his other drives to learn to cooperate (follow his instructions for love and fun) and compete (follow his instructions for power and freedom).

THE NEED TO SURVIVE

At birth, children become aware of pain and discomfort when their stomachs become too empty, their bottoms are too wet, they are deprived of touch from another human being for too long or they are lacking sleep. All the baby's behaviors, initially crying and wailing, are focused on communicating to the world: "Something is wrong! Fix it!"

THE NEED TO COOPERATE

From approximately eight months until 16 months, cooperative behaviors are the behaviors babies begin to learn will work to help them feel satisfied and full. Cooing, smiling, laughing, looking into their mother's eyes and following their father's movements result in the parent's staying close, feeding the baby with breast and companionship. Mother delights as baby smiles at her as she approaches. Father pridefully declares to all visitors that he can make baby laugh. Playing peek-a-boo with siblings and babysitters becomes a game that all look forward to. Baby learns that cooperative behaviors result in the match between the world he experiences with his hoped for good feeling in his internal, quality world.

THE NEED TO COMPETE

Then the child enters the "terrible twos." At this point, the child is beginning to learn that competitive behaviors are necessary to earn his own way. Yes, he is thirsty and wants some juice "BUT NOT FROM THE GREEN CUP. I WANT THE RED CUP!" If he only had the words to articulate this desire. Much to his mother's dismay, the toddler demands the world be his way by using the behaviors of cup throwing, crying, screaming and throwing himself onto the floor. Toddlers want choices, and they want to make their OWN decisions.

Spending any time around a child during this six-month period, all become aware that the feeling is much more competitive than cooperative. Baby learns that effective competitive behaviors help him get what he wants and successfully meet his needs.

EVOLVING AND REVOLVING CYCLES

What follows for the bulk of childhood is an ever evolving and revolving cycle. For approximately six months, a child concentrates his efforts on attempting and learning cooperative behaviors, meeting his cooperative needs. This is followed by an approximate period of six months when competitive behaviors are attempted and learned, meeting his competitive needs. With each subsequent cycle, even more cooperative behaviors are attempted and learned, followed by a cycle of more competitive behaviors attempted and learned. Although each cycle seems to be for approximately six months in early childhood, extending to one year from ages seven until adolescence, the predictable time and duration are less important than the revolution and evolution between these two periods of learning cooperative and competitive behaviors.

Why does this happen? From eight months to two years, a child feels satisfied because he has learned cooperative behaviors that allow him to meet his cooperative needs. During this time, he becomes more aware of the world. His ability to perceive the world has matured. The child becomes aware of more things in his environment that he wants to explore. Using his cooperative behaviors no longer works. This self-evaluation urges him to behave, driving the child to behave in competitive ways to grab hold of the newly discovered and expanding environment.

He is set into another cycle of approximately six months, this time concentrating on meeting his needs using competitive behaviors. Again during this time his ability to perceive the world matures. There is more of the world he wants to know, understand and explore. Using his competitive behaviors is no longer working to allow him to get close enough to learn and enjoy what he is exploring. So he shifts into another cycle where he concentrates on learning cooperative behaviors to meet his cooperative needs.

During the period when competitive behaviors are used more and more, the effective behavioral repertoire for meeting competitive needs increases. Self-evaluation for his competitive needs brings satisfaction and feelings of pleasure. But self-evaluation for cooperative needs that are not being met are perceived. Increased awareness and changes in perception of the larger world continue to evolve, shifting into a cycle of new and expanded cooperative behaviors being learned. Now the child is in a period when cooperative behaviors are used more and more, increasing the repertoire of effective cooperative behaviors for meeting cooperative needs. (See Table 6 below.)

TABLE 6

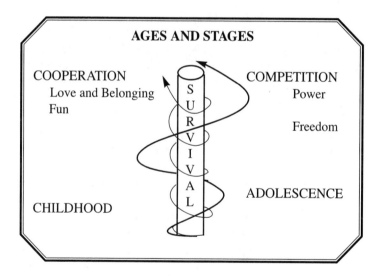

An example may help explain this process. An infant wants milk to relieve the pain in his stomach. He wants to survive. At eleven months, he cooperates with his mother and learns to drink milk from a cup, as well as from a bottle. He learns that cooperating with his mother allows him to experience a full tummy and the pride of learning the new and difficult behavior of drinking from a cup. At age two, he wants to use a cup to drink the milk. He wants to do this by himself, no longer needing or wanting his mother's assistance. His perception of the world has changed, so he can now discriminate between different kinds and colors of cups. Now he doesn't just want milk, nor does he just want milk in a cup. He realizes that milk tastes better in the red cup than in the green cup. He willfully demands the world to be his way.

Children need to learn to behave cooperatively enough to bring the world close enough to learn about it. Then children learn how to behave competitively to bend the world to meet their demands.

IN CHILDHOOD, SAFETY = COOPERATION

The child who is deep into the competitive stage does not abandon the cooperative drive and behaviors. The 18-month old child who visits the doctor's office with Mom may cling to Mom's leg for dear life. This is the same child who, thirty minutes before, argued with Mom, demanding his right to put his hat and mittens on by himself without any help from Mom. Even a child who is in a competitive phase will behave cooperatively when he is outside his safety zone. At home he feels safe enough to compete for his own way. At the strange, potentially unsafe environment of the doctor's office, this child knows that his safety depends on cooperating and sticking close to Mom.

A similar experience can occur even within the confines and safety of home. Mom and Dad return from their evening out, expecting to hear from the babysitter that life for all was one battle of wills after another. What a surprise when the babysitter reports how darling and charming their two-year old has been. Some parents begin to wonder if their child has been swapped for another. Others may fear that their parenting skills are in question. This darling and charming child behaves like a devil with them!

Driven by the need to survive, with the accompanying psychological aspect of safety, children will revert to cooperative behaviors when they feel unsafe or feel as if their survival is in doubt. So when our child is in a strange place or in the care of someone that he is unsure of, he will cooperate, even if he is in a competitive stage. Children must feel safe enough to behave competitively. Ultimately our child is driven to survive more strongly than he is driven to learn to compete. For children, co-operating with their care-giver equals their survival. Even though a child who is learning competitive behaviors may be more difficult to parent than when he is in his cooperative cycle, we can take that as an indication that our child feels safe and secure. He feels safe enough that he does not need to co-operate with us to know he will survive.

The six-month period of cooperative urges predominating, followed by another six months where competitive urges pre-dominate, continues through approximately the first seven years of a child's life. Then these "phases" begin to extend to eight, nine and ten-month periods, allowing for greater time periods to practice and learn either the increased cooperative or competitive behaviors.

PRE-ADOLESCENCE AND ADOLESCENCE

The child then enters pre-adolescence and finally ado-lescence. Some have been known to label these the "wonder years": it's a wonder parents and children can live through them together! It's the "terrible twos" all over again. Only now the child is older with a more mature perception of the world and with a greater repertoire of competitive behaviors. The competitive needs predominate, urging and driving behaviors. Adolescents want their own way. That is, they want to be treated like adults with all the privileges of adulthood, but they do not want to be responsible or held accountable for any of their behaviors. They want the power and freedom of adulthood and the fun and connections of childhood.

This is the period where not only is the parent's authority called into question, but so are her wisdom and knowledge. Understanding this time as the time where a child is individ-uating and separating can help to guide a parent as she creates an environment where her adolescent can successfully meet these needs and learn even more behaviors to meet his need for power and freedom effectively.

Even during this time of extreme use of competitive behaviors, the cooperative behaviors and cooperative urges are not gone. All teenagers look alike. Of course, this is an exaggeration. But they certainly look very similar to one another and look very different from most of their parents. Teenagers cooperate with one another and compete with their parents' generation. There is safety and power in numbers; the more of them that look the same, the greater the chance they will have some power within the adult society.

The cooperative and belonging aspect is not just with each other. Many adolescents want their teachers and parents to like them. They just don't want anyone to know this. It's not cool. Armed with this knowledge, parents can treat their children and their children's friends lovingly; without being too demonstrative!

Again, the parents' job is to help their child learn increasingly effective competitive behaviors. This can be tricky because often our child is competing with us, not wanting to listen or learn from us. But if we hold the keys to the car, we can teach our child the responsible behaviors he will need in order to receive permission from us to borrow our car. So, even though the child is urged by competitive feelings, we can behave cooperatively with the child to help him learn effective competitive behaviors, including competing with us.

Another change that occurs during adolescence is that competitive behaviors are the behaviors the adolescent now relies on when his safety is threatened. If a young person is faced with a situation where he is unsure of himself or others around him, he may choose to stand off and assess his situation or stand up to what he perceives as a threatening authority. If a young person feels safe, he will continue his cycle of behaving both cooperatively and competitively. If his safety is in question, the young person will now rely on competitive behaviors to feel safe. A feeling of safety, the psychological aspect of survival, is still the axis that determines successful evolution of both cooperative and competitive behaviors, but during adolescence the predominating drive is competitive.

The strong urge for meeting competitive needs is greatest in the early ages of adolescence. Around 16 years, luckily, the urge for cooperation begins to be felt and acted upon. By the later ages of adolescence, cooperative needs and behaviors are beginning to present almost an equal balance to the competitive needs and behaviors.

EARLY ADULTHOOD

By early adulthood, children have grown and matured, having learned a full complement of effective behaviors to meet both their competitive and cooperative needs They have learned enough effective behaviors now to enter the world and live happily and satisfactorily on their own. Pictures in the young adult's quality world continue to be created as well as the continuation of learning more about the world (perceptions continue to develop and be refined). So the cycles between cooperation and competition slow down greatly. Now it is not as easy for parents to recognize which phase their child is in. The young adult has learned enough effective behaviors to meet both cooperative and competitive urges. He can now enter the world, capable of surviving and living happily on his own.

Childhood is the time when a child is learning about himself and the world, including learning effective behaviors to satisfy both cooperative and competitive urges that arise from the psychological genetic instructions. In adolescence and early adulthood, a young person continues to experiment and learn effective behaviors to meet his basic needs. During this time a young person is also clarifying and creating more mature pictures in his quality world as well as his perceptions of the real world. Now as he approaches the time in life when he will be leaving his parent's home to make his own way in the world, he has learned enough about himself and the world and is capable of surviving. He is able to meet his other basic needs as well. He is ready and able to live without his parents.

A PARENT'S JOB

How does understanding the ages and stages of our children help in our job as parents?

Dad and his two sons, Mike, age 7 and Peter, age 5 are enjoying an afternoon at the park. Both boys are old enough to play on most of the equipment without needing a great deal of assistance from their dad. Dad is especially pleased to discover that Mike has decided that today is a day he will cooperate with everything his father says. Mike has shifted from a six-month stage of competing into a six-month stage of cooperating. Peter is not aware of this. He and his brother have been arguing and bickering relentlessly because both boys were in the competing phase together, and Peter still is. Everything that Mike does is followed by his saying, "Hey Dad, look at me," or "Hey Dad, watch this."

As I've already said, Peter is still very much in his competing phase. So as Mike clamors for Dad's attention more and more, Peter is feeling like he is losing power over his father's attention. Whatever Mike does, Peter is right behind, trying to do the same, only better. The problem is that Peter is two years younger and two years smaller than his brother. So he never feels like he wins. Mike is happy to have his brother follow him around as if he is playing follow the leader, with Mike being the leader. Dad is happy to watch his boys play together although he has an uneasy feeling. There is something bothering Peter, but Dad just can't figure out what. When Mike climbs to the top of the jungle gym, Dad sees Peter clambering behind.

He calls to Peter, "Don't go up to where your brother is. It's too high and there isn't enough room."

Peter, feeling furious, calls back, "I can, too."

"No," his father says sternly. "In fact, Mike why don't you come down so Peter won't feel tempted."

Mike, being the wonderfully cooperative child that he is, does as his father asks. When both boys return to the safety of firm ground, Dad decides to offer another alternative for fun.

"Let's go over to the ball field and play some kick ball," he suggests.

"Okay," both boys agree. Mike's agreement is based on his cooperative spirit, wanting to be part of the group having fun together. Peter agrees because he thinks he can win.

As the kick ball game begins, Dad plays permanent pitcher. Each boy, in turn, gets up to kick and score runs while the other boy plays first base/fielder. The game seems to be progressing well with all seeming to have a good time. Peter is up for the last inning. He needs to score one more run to tie with his brother, twice more to win. With all his concentration and all his effort, he approaches a good pitch that he knows he can kick a mile. As he runs to the ball, he kicks so hard that he over-kicks the ball, missing it completely and falls to the ground hard, landing on his rear end. Mike and his father both begin laughing. It was a funny sight. Peter, furious, begins screaming, ranting and raving about the bad pitch his father gave him to set him up to lose, how Mike had really cheated when he was up, and how he hated both his father and brother forever. All of this was mostly incoherent because it is all said through his sobbing tears of anger.

When Dad and Mike realize how angry and upset Peter is, their laughter immediately stops, but it is too late. Peter is hurt, angry and humiliated. The moment that he was sure was going to lead to his victory and power for the afternoon, instead ended in defeat. All three return home in silence. Dad feels particularly disappointed. The ending of the afternoon seemed to spoil any good feelings or good time that had come from the afternoon.

Later that night when he tucks Peter into bed, he tells his son how sorry he is that the afternoon had been spoiled. "I'm sorry I hurt your feelings by laughing at you, Peter," he tells his son. "You had been playing so well all through the game. I can't believe how much better you are playing these days. Especially your fielding. Anybody who can hold his older brother to a one run lead is a pretty good player, I'd say." Dad had said all the right things to Peter.

"I am getting pretty good, aren't I, Dad? Next time we play, I bet I win."

"It will sure be a good contest, I bet," his father says.

This brief story tells of the two different "attitudes" of two different children, both living in the same family. Mike was in his cooperative phase, and so was willing to go along and get along. Peter, being driven by his instruction for power and freedom dominating, was part of the group, but his feelings about the activities were different. Both boys were able to behave in ways that met their needs. Even though Peter didn't win as he had hoped, he still was able to behave powerfully and freely without hurting anyone else. Dad was able to intervene, when necessary, to keep the boys safe, and because he was a loving, verbal Dad, was able to help Peter evaluate his kickball skills to discover increased power, even if it didn't result in beating his brother in the game.

Things get a little trickier and potentially more difficult when both children are in the competitive cycle at the same time. Since power and freedom are the instructions driving them, and often this means power over and freedom from their sibling, parents can feel particularly challenged. Often a parent is the object of the children's competition, as well. The older child can seem to have the upper hand because he is frequently physically stronger, bigger and has mastered more developmental tasks, but even younger children learn how to power over their older brother or sister. Sometimes they provoke their sibling into mischief and then report to their parent what their sibling has done in an effort to have their parent "punish" the older child. Sometimes the younger child exaggerates a painful cry, so the parent will intervene to protect the younger child. We need to understand that part of what is occurring is that our child is growing and developing through either cooperative or competitive phases in an attempt to follow his genetic instructions to meet his basic needs. Even though our child may be in a predominant competitive stage, he still has the urge to behave cooperatively (and vice versa). During the competitive stage, the drive to compete is the strongest and the one the child acts on the most frequently, but the cooperative needs are still driving the child to meet the cooperative needs as well. Though we may have two children, both in the competitive stage, we can still appeal to their cooperative need-fulfillment when attempting to resolve their differences.

INCREASED OPPORTUNITIES

Understanding our child's ages and stages may give us clues to ways we can help our child grow and mature. Even though I have described these stages as a six-month time schedule, our child does not look to a calendar then move to a different stage of cooperation or competition. Our child will tell us which stage he is in through his behavior.

If we notice that the kinds of interactions we're having most frequently with our child seem to be more aggravating, more confrontational, more of a tug-of-war we can suspect that our child is in a competitive phase of his development. He is driven to meet his needs for more power and more freedom by learning more effective competitive behaviors. Our job is to help him follow these instructions successfully so we can increase the amount of freedom and power opportunities available to our child. If we don't, he will still be driven to behave competitively. Without other options to meet his need, he will compete with us.

When our two-year old demands more, argues with us more and cooperates less, we should offer him more options. Does he want to eat his supper with a spoon or a fork? Does he want to use the crayons or his markers when coloring? Keeping in mind the appropriate choices for his age, we want to offer opportunities, but not so many that our child becomes overwhelmed by them.

A seven-year old may be in his competitive phase, arguing with us about his bedtime (even though this is something we have all agreed upon). Next he complains about the school lunch we pack for him. Finally he tells us that we never let him do any of the fun things his friends are allowed to do. At this point, we should suspect that he is behaving to meet a competitive need and review with him all that is presently available to him to help him meet his needs for power and freedom. We ask him to help us increase these opportunities through our combined suggestions. Allowing him to complain and then working together to find acceptable solutions, provides another opportunity for him to meet his needs for power and freedom.

During those times when we notice our child is a dream come true and a pleasure to live with, pay attention to what is happening. He is probably in his cooperative stage. These are the times when we can do no wrong in his eyes. Because he has such a strong need to cooperate, he overlooks all our shortcomings. However, we can still work with our child to create additional opportunities for him to meet his cooperative needs. These are the wonderful times when we can help our child learn how to accomplish successful completion of a chore or learn a new task. He is anxious to please and willing to learn. Provide him with as many opportunities as you can to help him learn and grow, being sure that they are age appropriate.

SAFE AND SECURE

Remember too, the biological need for survival with the accompanying psychological feeling of safety must prevail in our child's environment in order for him to learn effective cooperative and competitive behaviors. If our child is not feeling safe, he will rely on cooperative behaviors to help him feel safe. If our adolescent does not feel safe, he will rely on competitive behaviors to help him feel safe.

Certainly we all want our children to feel as safe and secure as possible all of the time, but there are times when safety is in question: natural disasters, weather catastrophes, death of a loved one or violence in the community, to name a few. A parent's job is to return a sense of safety to the child's life as quickly as possible. In so doing, a parent has returned the environment to optimum conditions for the child to continue learning and developing. Feeling safe, he will be able to continue to learn the full complement of behaviors to move successfully toward independence.

SUMMARY

• Basic needs and genetic instructions enable a child's survival and his learning the behaviors necessary to live independent of parents eventually.

• Cooperative and competitive behaviors are the two halves of the whole complement of all of the behaviors necessary for independent life. Behaviors derive from needs. The psychological needs are complementary needs.

• Fun and love are the cooperative needs. We need to learn effective cooperative behaviors to meet the needs for love and fun.

• Power and freedom are the competitive needs. We need to learn effective competitive behaviors to meet the needs for power and freedom successfully.

• Safety, the psychological feeling accompanying the need to survive, is the axis that the other needs evolve around.

• From eight months through the rest of childhood, children enter cycles of approximately six months in duration of intense learning of the cooperative and competitive behaviors necessary to follow all of their genetic instructions.

• A child enters a six-month cycle of learning cooperative behaviors to meet cooperative needs, then a six-month cycle of learning competitive behaviors to meet competitive needs. During each of these six-month cycles, the child's ability to perceive and understand the world also changes and matures. These six-month revolving and evolving cycles continue until the child reaches pre-adolescence.

• In childhood, a child will rely on cooperative behaviors, no matter what six-month cycle he is in, if his safety and security is threatened.

• During pre-adolescence and adolescence, the competitive needs are driving the young person's behavior most strongly. The cooperative needs are not abandoned. There is a greater emphasis on cooperation with peers than with parents, though.

• During adolescence, the young person will rely on competitive behaviors when his sense of safety or security is threatened.

• During young adulthood a greater balance exists between the cooperative needs and the competitive needs. Now the young person has learned the full complement of effective behaviors to meet all of his needs. He is now capable of independent living.

• Understanding the child's developmental cycles allows a parent to provide increased opportunities for the child to learn effective competitive behaviors when he is in the competitive stage and cooperative behaviors when he is in the cooperative stage. Observing the child's most frequent kinds of behaviors will let the parent know which stage the child is in.

• Even when the child is in the competitive stage, the cooperative needs still exist. A parent can appeal to the co-operative needs in attempting to resolve disputes.

• A feeling of safety must be the prevailing environment for a child in order for him to learn the effective cooperative and competitive behaviors.

Chapter Seven
Meeting Our Own Needs as People and as Parents

AGES AND STAGES CONTINUED

We are ready to continue our discussion of ages and stages by extending the growth and development that occur during adulthood. As was discussed in the previous chapter, childhood and young adulthood are the times when we learn effective behaviors to satisfy our complementary needs of cooperation and competition. Our genetic instructions drive us to meet these needs and learn the behaviors that will satisfy them. We experience cycles where the cooperative needs of love, belonging and fun drive us to behave in effective ways to satisfy these needs. This is followed by a competitive cycle where power and freedom drive us to learn effective behaviors to satisfy these needs. The six-month cycle during early childhood extends to approximately ten months until early adolescence. Then, in adolescence, this cycle slows down so that the competitive drives for freedom and power remain the dominant needs, ensuring the young person will learn the effective behaviors to survive on her own in adulthood. Remember though, that even during a cycle where the competitive needs dominate the behaviors, the cooperative needs are also present, driving a person to behave to satisfy these needs as well.

MORE BALANCE

The continuous evolution of cooperative and competitive needs driving behavior continues into and during adulthood. However, these patterns are neither so distinct, nor easily identified. Even when one kind of need dominates, the other is strongly present. During adulthood the needs drive our behavior in more of a balanced cycle.

The predominant need for cooperation in adulthood can be seen in the drive to form strong and long-term loving relationships. During this time "coupling" occurs. For some, this translates into developing long-term marital relationships. Simultaneously there is the competitive drive to make a place for oneself within the society. This means becoming educated and trained in a profession. Thus, during adulthood, from approximately age 20 through 40, people are involved in satisfying cooperative and competitive needs.

For some people, one of these drives feels stronger and thus is the need that is focused on. For women, the cooperative needs often predominate. So a woman may begin her career but focuses on marrying, birthing and raising a family. Often men will marry and sire children, but concern focuses behaviors on the competitive drive of "making it" in their stated professions. Even though both genders are driven by all of their basic genetic needs, the focus of their energy and attention may be different.

In mid-life a change occurs. This is often the time that people take stock of their lives and re-establish priorities. For some, this means pursuing those things not pursued before, focusing greater attention and behaviors on the complementary needs less attended to previously. Women may begin to pursue more competitive, career-minded goals. Men may begin to devote less energy on their careers and spend more time pursuing hobbies or re-connecting with mates, friends and family. Thus, the cooperative need becomes a greater focus for men during this time. Greater balance and complementarity of the genetic needs occur over the whole of a lifetime.

The cycle of the complementary needs that predominates does not necessarily fall along gender lines. Certainly there are examples of women who spend time, attention and drive to compete in the work world, just as there are examples of men who connect and focus a great deal of time and attention on developing and maintaining life-long relationships as their priority during the ages of 20 to 40. I do not mean to imply that we are genetically driven to behave competitively or cooperatively based on our gender. There are also increasing examples of both men and women who diligently behave to "have it all": happy, satisfying family lives and successful, fulfilling careers. An understanding that we all are born with the genetic instructions that drive our behaviors for love, fun, power and freedom is indicated by a life that contains activities, relationships and focus on many quality world pictures that represent all of the basic needs.

Generally speaking, however, people live within a limited amount of time and energy. So one-half of the complementary needs become a greater drive and focus during adulthood, just as it was during adolescence. Instead of this cycle's being ten years in duration as it was during adolescence, it extends to 20 years. Because we have learned increasingly effective behaviors to meet all of our needs, we can satisfy our cooperative needs effectively enough during this 20-year cycle, so that we can focus more intense attention on the competitive needs that we feel are driving us the hardest. Or we may have learned enough effective competitive behaviors to satisfy those needs, so we can focus most of our attention on the cooperative needs. During mid-life we enter another 20-year cycle where our intense attention is driven by the other complementary half of our needs not previously attended to as fully. (See Table 7 below.)

Table 7

AGES AND STAGES

COOPERATION — Love and Belonging, Fun

COMPETITION — Power

SURVIVAL

Freedom
LATER
ADULTHOOD

ADULTHOOD

CHILDHOOD

ADOLESCENCE

PARENTING AND MORE

Becoming a parent is a behavior that some choose to satisfy basic genetic instructions. For some this choice is thoughtfully and purposefully made. Others become parents as a consequence of following a biological survival instruction to procreate and the fun drive of enjoying sex with the surprising consequence of becoming a parent. No matter how the decision to have children occurs, becoming a parent is a potentially need-satisfying circumstance. Learning to be a good parent is a quality world picture for most parents and obviously the focus of this book. As parents, we need to learn to satisfy our own needs without interfering with our children's satisfying their own needs. This is true for people who became parents even when this was not a conscious or planned event. Parenting certainly can be an effective need-satisfying behavior for both parent and child. We also need to learn how to follow our genetic instructions and meet our needs, not only as parents, but in other ways, too. Our lives with our children certainly can and should be a quality world picture, but not our only one.

🏠　　🏠　　🏠　　🏠

Elizabeth, a single mother of 14-year old Jason, returns home from a frustrating day of work. An important deadline was missed because two of the people in her department refused to double check an essential stage in the project. She had reminded them, but apparently they ignored her. When she walks into her house after having stopped at the grocery store to purchase what she would prepare for the evening meal, she discovers the radio on full volume, her son's school backpack in its usual spot in the middle of the kitchen floor, and her son nowhere to be found. Once again he has not left her a note letting her know where he is and when she can expect him home. An hour later he returns.

"What's for dinner?" is his greeting to his mother.

"Where have you been? Once again there was no note for me," is her response. His mother goes on to recite the evening's menu.

"I hate fish! Why don't you ever remember I hate fish?" Jason complains.

This last comment is more than Elizabeth can handle. She blows up, screaming at him and calling him names that she wouldn't use against her worst enemy. Jason returns the raging phrases, increasing the intensity by using language that he knows his mother finds particularly offensive. The battle ends with Elizabeth banishing Jason to his room, where he retreats with pleasure and relief. His backpack remains unmoved in the middle of the kitchen floor.

Jason's day at school was unusually powerless for him as well. He was ready for a confrontation when he saw his mother. As he sits in his room, listening to music on his headphones, he feels some relief from the day's frustration but also dreads the long lonely evening where he and his mother will probably remain silent enemies.

🏠　　🏠　　🏠　　🏠

Sounds pretty frustrating and bleak, doesn't it? Neither Elizabeth nor Jason is behaving in effective ways to meet any of their needs. Both happen to be in a strong competitive developmental cycle with the drive for power being the greatest for both of them. Neither was able to behave in effective powerful ways during the course of the day, so both were "loaded for bear" before they even encountered one another. Now each of them is attempting to power over the other, each hoping to feel more powerful. But powering over another, even when it is effective for meeting the need for power temporarily, usually keeps the need for love and belonging from being met effectively.

"WHAT DO I NEED?"

Because she is the parent, it is Elizabeth's job to learn more effective behaviors to meet her need for power before she begins her interaction with Jason. Ideally she would be able to take the time to self-evaluate that she is feeling powerless and needs to behave in ways to meet her need for power before she gets home. This doesn't mean she should yell at the grocery store clerk or cut other drivers off on her trip home. It may mean that she stops some place quiet on her way home, where she can think and plan what her strategy will be for her next day at work. Perhaps she can talk with a colleague or supervisor before she even leaves work to see if she can manage the project in ways that help her gain more power and recognition. Even if Elizabeth makes no plans for how she will handle her work problems, she needs to recognize that she is feeling particularly powerless before she gets home. In so doing, she has increased her awareness that she might be more likely to attempt to power over Jason because she hasn't felt very powerful during the day at work. With this knowledge she can plan a strategy for behaving powerfully without using or abusing Jason to meet this need. For some people, planning and cooking an evening meal can be a powerful experience. If this is true for Elizabeth, taking the time to realize what she needs and what she plans to do to follow this drive effectively, decreases the likelihood that she will use her relationship with Jason as a means to satisfy her genetic power drive.

Once Elizabeth has contemplated her own situation, she is ready to interact with Jason. She will be a parent who will work with her son to help him meet his needs. Because she has evaluated her own needs and instructions within the context of her work life, she has decreased the chance that she will use her son in a way that will keep him from meeting his needs. As parents and adults who have a larger repertoire of effective behaviors, our job is to recognize our own internal self-evaluative signals that tell us that we are not getting what we want and need. With that information we must meet our own needs, so we can then be available to help our children learn effective behaviors to meet their needs.

Armed with the information about herself, Elizabeth is now ready to interact with Jason. This doesn't mean that she will be happy about coming home and finding the radio left on, her son absent without a note informing her of his where-abouts or his backpack abandoned in the middle of the kitchen floor. This scene will probably still produce feelings of displeasure for Elizabeth, telling her that what she wants and what she is getting are two different things. She will still be driven to behave. But her behavior will not include the double whammy of feeling powerless from work. In fact, because she has taken the time for self-reflection and self-evaluation, she may be more sensitive to her desire to power over Jason, thus helping to temper her potential tantrum.

Aware that she is in a more competitive cycle in her own development and aware that Jason is as well, Elizabeth can formulate her strategy of how she will approach Jason when he returns home. What can she do to increase his sense of freedom and power in this situation? Elizabeth may become aware that her intense focus on power at work has also increased her need to connect and feel lovingly toward her son to balance all of her needs. She may realize that helping Jason learn how to meet his needs effectively for power and freedom will actually help her feel greater freedom and increased power.

📖   📖   📖   📖

"Hello Jason. I missed you when I got home. Where have you been?" Elizabeth greets her son.

"I went over to Kelly's house. He got a new computer game we were playing with," Jason answers.

"I would appreciate a note next time, so I know where you are and when I can expect you. Did you have fun?"

"Yeah, the game is great. It's kind of aggravating, though, because Kelly knows the game so well he beat me every time." Jason may be giving his mother a hint about his sense of powerlessness as well.

"Help me get our supper ready, would you? Putting your school things away would be great."

"What are we having for supper?" Jason asks as he puts his backpack away.

"Fish," his mother answers.

"I hate fish, Mom. Why don't you ever remember that?"

"It looked good and is easy to prepare. I had a terribly frustrating day at work, so I was anxious to find something simple to make for dinner. How about if you choose what we will have for tomorrow night?" Elizabeth is honestly letting Jason know why she chose what she did even though it may not be to his liking. But

she is attempting to give him more power and freedom in planning the meals.

"I had a terrible day, too," Jason tells his mother. "I was hoping for something really good to eat to help with this yucky day."

"Well, how about if we go out to eat tonight instead of waiting until Friday. That way we can talk about our awful day and each choose what we want from a menu. We'll eat the fish tomorrow night."

Jason nods in agreement.

"But we won't be able to go out to eat tonight and Friday night, Jason. Our budget can't afford that."

"Okay," he agrees.

"Maybe we can help each other out tonight so that we can both have a better day tomorrow," Elizabeth suggests.

At some point during this evening or in the next few days, Elizabeth can remind Jason of a few of the house rules. Together they can re-establish leaving notes when either is not home to inform the other of their where-abouts, turning off all appliances, including the radio before leaving the house, as well as putting backpacks and briefcases away when returning home. Of course, this won't be new information for this 14-year old boy, but Elizabeth is keeping his age and stage in the forefront of her mind, knowing he is wanting greater power and freedom, including power in making house rules and freedom from rules that she alone established. She is less aware of her own age and stage but is aware of her increased need for power. Elizabeth is continually learning how to behave in ways that will help both Jason and her have power together. She is meeting her own needs, thus enabling her to be available to her son to help him meet his needs. This, in turn, helps her meet her needs as well.

MEETING NEEDS, BUT NOT AT THE OTHER'S EXPENSE

As parents, we must learn to meet our own needs without interfering with our child's meeting her needs. This is an issue that is constantly before parents. As humans, parents are driven by psychological needs as well. We behave in the world to satisfy our genetic instructions. Our job as humans, to meet our basic needs, includes parenting in need satisfying ways. How can we, as parents, balance our own need-satisfaction while also helping our child meet her needs? This is a subtle and tricky issue because parenting is one of the effective behaviors we use to satisfy our needs. When we parent in ways that allow only us to meet our needs and that interfere with our child's meeting her needs, we have erred.

How can we decide if what we are doing is only for our own benefit? One way is to inventory our lives based on our basic needs. How do I meet my need for love and belonging, for fun, for power, for freedom? Does my list include activities, people and places exclusive of my child? Is my child on the list? If the only loving relationship I have in my life is the one with my child, then there is a greater potential that I am meeting my needs and interfering with my child's meeting her needs. Does my list of fun, satisfying behaviors not include my child? If this is true, then there may be a greater potential that I am attempting to meet my needs and interfering with my child's meeting her needs. If our list includes our child and our parenting job but is not exclusive to our child and our job as a parent, then chances are good that we have a wide variety of alternatives for need fulfillment as a person and as a parent. (See Table 4, page 96 for guidance.)

Depending on her age, we can also ask our child to inventory her life based on the basic needs. If our child is old enough to talk, then she is old enough to participate in this activity with us. Asking her who she loves and who she feels loves her, where she feels important and recognized, where and when she has fun, and where she feels she has choices, are questions that will help us discover how our child is meeting her needs. For very young children, her answers will probably include us most frequently. As our child gets older, however, more and more people, places and activities hopefully will be included. Again, including us, but not exclusively, will give us a good assessment of how effectively our child is meeting her needs. This inventory can indicate how successfully our child is meeting her needs without our needs' interfering with her.

PARENTS ARE HUMAN, TOO

I had just arrived home in the late afternoon from a trip to the grocery store. My 15-year old son, David, greeted me at the door.

"Don't go anywhere. Paul is in the emergency room of the hospital. He might need a ride home from you. Ned was driving them to McDonald's and was in a car accident. No one was seriously hurt although Jimmy banged his chin on the front seat, biting his lip. The cops sent them to the hospital to make sure everybody was okay. Steve just called asking if Paul and I can go with him to a Pawtucket Red Sox game tonight. He'll drive us. Can we go?"

What a greeting. After getting more of the details of all that transpired from David, I had to make a decision about my two sons traveling 35 miles from home, through city traffic, with a fairly new driver. David was pressuring me for an answer immediately because Steve was going to call back soon and needed to know if Paul and David would be joining him.

"David, I would rather wait until your father gets home before I give you an answer. Can you wait?" I knew that if I answered him immediately, it would be based on my fear of the car accident Paul was just in. I knew my answer would be no because I wanted to keep my sons safe and close to home. I was aware that I was answering from my own needs. I wanted additional time and a second opinion from my husband to help me make our decision.

"How long before Dad gets home?" David wanted to know. He was pressing for an answer.

"I don't know how long he will be," I answered. "Can you wait?"

"I guess I'll have to," David answered.

An hour later Paul returned home, delivered by Ned's mother. All were okay, including the man driving the car that Ned hit. Ned's car was banged up, but no one was hurt.

"Mom, we need an answer. Steve is going to call any minute." David was still pressing for permission to go to the game.

"If I have to give you an answer now, David, then my answer is no," I told my son.

"You're just saying that because Paul was in an accident and you're scared. If we asked you yesterday, you would have said yes," David astutely pointed out my thinking.

"You're right, David. I am scared. I don't know what my answer would have been if Paul hadn't been in a car accident. I'm not so sure I would have easily given you a yes answer. I think the four of us need to sit down and talk about the guidelines of where you go with your friends who are new drivers. I wanted to wait for your father to give you an answer, so I wouldn't be answering you based on my fear. But he's not home. So I am answering you based on my fear."

In the above scene I was meeting my own needs for safety first. I may have been interfering with my sons' meeting their needs for freedom and fun, but I could not think of another way to meet my need for safety and survival besides keeping them out of a car driven by a new, inexperienced driver, who was going to travel through city traffic, far from home. Both David and I were aware that my decision was affected by the car accident Paul had just been in. We both knew I was meeting my need first. Luckily, this does not happen frequently, so even though David was not happy with my decision, he accepted it. I wonder if he, too, was feeling a little shaky about his own safety, based on Paul's recent experience. I knew that even if that were the case, there was no way a 15-year old boy was going to admit his fears and doubts to his mother. This private information was his to control as he wanted.

Our job, as parents, is to meet our own needs with and without our children. Our job as parents is to help our children learn to meet their needs with and without us. During times in our lives when our needs are not effectively met, we need to learn effective behaviors to meet our needs. We should not use our children as our means to meet our needs, however.

A parent who punishes his daughter because she did not have a good soccer practice or a parent who insists that his son apply to his alma mater prep school or a parent who insists that his child take piano lessons when the child wants to take flute lessons, needs to examine whose needs are being met. Our job, as parents, is to provide our children with opportunities to meet their needs, including providing them with additional information about the world that the child may not have. When we insist that our child behave in ways to satisfy our quality world pictures, we are attempting to meet our needs through our child's behavior. There will be times when following this guideline may not seem possible. Being aware of those times when we direct our child's behavior to meet our own needs allows us the opportunity to share that information with our child. If this is something we do relatively infrequently, our child will accept it. Sharing this information helps our child feel less manipulated. It also allows us increased awareness so that we can attempt to correct and learn different, more effective behaviors for the future. We can plan how and where we can meet our own needs without using our child to do so.

CLASHING COMPETITIVE CYCLES

There will be times when parents' development and their child's development seem to clash. During the child's adolescence, a parent may be facing a new shift into greater energy and focus on meeting his competitive needs, for example. The adults, the parents, have the responsibility of learning how to honor their own growth and development while facilitating and guiding their child in her growth and development. Clashes may still occur, but with increased awareness and knowledge, both parent and child can learn more effective ways to compete cooperatively so that fewer clashes may occur in the future.

SUMMARY

• During our lives as adults, we continue the cycle of cooperative and competitive stages, but these stages are more balanced.

- From age 20 to 40, an adult will focus much energy on either the cooperative or competitive needs. During midlife, adults will assess their lives and then spend the next 20 years focusing on the other, complementary needs.
- Parenting is a quality world picture and behavior for some adults. Parenting can be a need fulfilling behavior for both parent and child.
- Parents should be sure they are not meeting their needs at their child's expense, resulting in the child's inability to meet her needs. During a family upset, if a parent can meet his needs before approaching the child, the parent is less likely to meet a need by interfering with the child's ability to meet her needs. A parent can accomplish this by stepping back and asking himself, "What do I need? How will I get it?" Then he is able to approach the child.
- Parents should meet their needs in ways that include their job of parenting and their child, not exclusive to their parenting job and their child.
- By asking a child to do a needs inventory a parent can also assess if the parent is interfering with the child's ability to meet her needs.
- There may be times when a parent meets his needs and interferes with his child's ability to meet her needs. What helps this situation is if it occurs infrequently. If the parent is aware that this is happening, he can apologize and also make a better plan for the future.
- The parent's development and the child's development may clash with one another. Because the parent is the adult, with more experience and a greater ability to meet his needs because of his larger behavioral repertoire, it is the parent's job to figure out how to honor his own self-growth and not interfere with his child's ability to learn and grow.

Chapter Eight
Peaceful Disciplining

Paul and David are 3-1/2 years old. It is a late spring morning, with some warmth in the air. The boys are outside playing in their sandbox. I've momentarily left them, knowing they can happily occupy themselves there for hours. I run inside the house and collect all the wet clean laundry into a basket. I hang clothes on the line to dry, only a few yards from the boys, with my back to them. I vaguely hear their happy voices in the background, but I'm lost somewhere in my own thoughts. A familiar sound pulls me back into awareness of my surroundings and to the boys. They have turned the hose on and pulled it into the sandbox with them. I quickly move to shut off the water, running to the sandbox to collect the nozzle and maneuver the hose out of the sandbox. My motion is fast enough to prevent most of the sand from becoming a soggy mess. Only one corner is wet. If the boys add just enough dry sand, perfect mud pies can be made. I explain to the boys that having the turned-on hose in the sandbox is against the rules. Four brown eyes look up at me with what I take for recognition.

I drag the hose back toward the house, close to my clothesline and return to my task of hanging wet laundry out to dry. With that chore complete, I tell Paul and David I'm going inside to make their lunch, asking them to stay within the yard area, including the sandbox, telling them I'll come collect them soon, and we'll wash up for lunch.

In the kitchen I again lose myself in my own thoughts and am again drawn back to present consciousness by the familiar sound of water running somewhere in the house. It doesn't take me long to recognize the sound as water running through the hose. Because of the distance I must travel, my move to turn

*off the hose, reach the sandbox and toss the nozzle out of
the enclosure is not quick enough to save any of the sand
from wetness. The boys' happy laughter changes to
hushed silence. They are wet from head to toe, sand
stuck in hair, fingers, shoes and inside of socks. My
anger seeps through my silence.*

*"Follow me," I command. They do as they are told.
Each boy is directed to sit on the stone stoop outside of
the back door. I remove shoes, peel off socks, pull shirts
over heads and drop shorts onto the stone, so they are
wearing only underpants.*

*"Inside, both of you, and sit in the brown chairs. We
need to talk about this, but I'm going to rinse your
clothes our first," I direct in a stern voice. Both boys are
familiar with the "brown chairs" as these have been
used as time out chairs all of their lives. I take the time
to repair some of the damage that has been done to
their clothes, not because it is so severe, but so that I
can use the time away from them as my own time out. I
need to figure out what to do. I want to approach them
without anger. Rinsing and shaking sand from clothes
provides me with the thinking and planning time I need.*

"Boys, what did you do?" I ask.

*"We played with the hose in the sandbox," David
replies.*

*"And what was the rule?" I ask. "No hose in the
sandbox," Paul answers.*

"So, you broke the rule?" I ask. Both boys nod.

*"Okay, so something has to happen," I explain. "A
consequence. Since you couldn't follow the rules of
playing outside, you'll need to play in your room after
lunch. Do you understand?" I ask. Again both boys
nod.*

*"Okay, let's get washed up and put on dry clothes for
lunch."*

*At the end of the meal, David asks "Can we have
dessert, Mom?"*

"What's the rule, David?"

*"If we eat our meal, we can have one sweet a day,"
he explains.*

*"Have you eaten your meal?" I ask. He nods.
"Have you had any other sweets today?" He shakes his
head no. "So can you have dessert?"*

*"Yeah, but what about the hose in the sandbox?" he
asks, eyes opened wide.*

*"The sandbox has nothing to do with dessert," I
explain. "You've followed the plan around dessert, so
dessert you shall have."*

*After lunch and the usual thirty minutes of Sesame
Street, the boys march upstairs to their bedroom for play
time. I remain downstairs reading. Twenty minutes
later David calls to me from the top of the stairs.*

Standing at the bottom of the stairs I ask, "Yes?"

"We're having fun, is that okay?"

*"Yes, David. You can have fun, you just can't play
outside for awhile."*

*As I return to my reading, I wonder who is learning
the most about rules, consequences and discipline.*

AN ART, NOT A SCIENCE

The ultimate goal of disciplining anyone is to help that
person learn to discipline himself. We can begin by shifting
our thinking about discipline to that of a teaching activity,
where we teach our child the effective behavior of self-discipline. This first step will help in creating peace, ours and our
child's. By teaching our child self-discipline, we will move
toward the ultimate goal of parenting: teaching our children to
live responsible, creative, fulfilling lives, independent of us, but
hopefully still involved with us.

Teaching self-discipline is not an exact science. That is
why using any disciplinary approach does not work 100
percent of the time. Teaching self-discipline is an art. As a
parent we get to practice this art on a daily basis. Depending
on the age and stage of our child, it may be on an hourly basis.
As we grow to understand the basic principles of teaching self-
discipline, we will practice this art like an artist. That is,
occasionally we will create works of breath-taking beauty.
Other times we will muddle with the paint so much that all we
have is a big, brown, indistinct mess. Being a parent means we

are working with a living, growing, changing canvas. As long as we practice peaceful discipline lovingly, what we create will be wonderful and forgiving of the mistakes we make.

RESPONSIBILITY

Although people are born with the drive to behave to satisfy a basic need, we are not born knowing behaviors. We begin learning effective behaviors that will satisfy our genetic instructions as children and continue this learning process throughout our lives. In addition to learning effective behaviors, we also learn values and morals. Parents teach their children values and morals and behaviors that are not only effective in following the human genetic instructions, but also those behaviors that are acceptable and exemplary of these values and morals. Each family determines its values and morals based on pictures in family members' quality world. (For many, this also includes teaching the family's religious beliefs.) I do not intend to advocate any values or morals for families, save one: responsibility.

Responsibility, as I am defining it, means behaving in ways that enable a person to follow her genetic instructions and meet her needs and do not interfere with any other person's meeting his needs. There is a good deal of religious and ethical writings and teachings that support and advocate this idea. A great deal of psychological reasoning and rationale support this concept as well. We have all learned about "survival of the fittest" from basic biology. More recently there has been increased scientific research discussing an idea of cooperation among and between species, as well as within species, to support survival of the group (reminiscent of the complementary needs of cooperation and competition). I am suggesting that all parents (as well as all people) accept the value in this definition of responsibility. Living responsibly means behaving in ways that allow a person to meet her needs without interfering with another person's meeting his needs.

The concept of responsibility is an external value. We must learn and then adopt this value as part of our quality world picture of how we want to behave in the world and how we want others in the world to behave. Because responsibility is an external concept, a parent's job is to teach the child how to behave responsibly. Children are not born with this value or this ability. Children are born with an urge to behave to meet their psychological needs. There is no part of a child's system that urges him to behave responsibly. A parent is the teacher and guide in helping her child learn this.

EXPECT MISTAKES AS PART OF LEARNING

Because children are not born with the knowledge of responsibility, nor the ability to behave responsibly, they will make mistakes, sometimes misbehaving or behaving irresponsibly. As a parent, we should expect and accept this. A parent can decrease her own frustration, approaching her child as a calm and peaceful teacher, knowing that a normal part of learning includes mistakes and errors. Learning how to behave responsibly and effectively continues, even when the child reaches adolescence and young adulthood. Each age and stage has new tasks and challenges. But throughout, we are teaching our children how to behave effectively and responsibly. So teenagers will also misbehave and behave irresponsibly (making mistakes) as they test the limits and boundaries of meeting their needs without interfering with others' meeting needs. Part of our child's job is to learn to live responsibly. Our job is to guide and teach our child how, by teaching him self-discipline. When a child (or any person) learns effective behaviors to meet his needs without interfering with other people meeting their needs he has learned self-discipline, behaving responsibly, independently and interdependently.

FREEDOM AND SAFETY

Reviewing and expanding our discussion on the genetic needs for freedom and safety (a psychological aspect of survival) will help us understand how we will teach our child to behave responsibly, ultimately learning the behavior of self-discipline. The genetic instruction for freedom means a drive for options, opportunities and choices. As humans, we want enough options, opportunities and choices to meet our other needs for safety, love, power and fun. We are driven by an urge to have enough freedeom, but not more than we feel we can handle. When a person has too much freedom, she may begin to feel unsafe, seeking boundaries or limits to freedom in order to feel safe. If a person has too many limits, she may feel safe, but then her urge for freedom feels restricted. When either too much or too little freedom exists, poor behavioral choices may result, as a person attempts either to feel safer or feel more free. Some examples may help illustrate this point.

TOO MUCH FREEDOM, TOO LITTLE SAFETY

When a two-year old child is given the freedom to play in a relative's den without an adult present to help this child understand what is safe to play with and what is unsafe, the child may run helter-skelter throughout the den, exploring everything and anything within reach and beyond. If, after awhile, an adult still does not enter the room to let the child know he is not alone, the child may begin literally to climb on the furniture, up the wall, across the ceiling and come down the other wall. The child does not know the limits. None have been set for him. He is looking to find limits so that he can feel safe.

Some of us may know children like this. Essentially their parents have said to this child, the world is your oyster, go for it. Probably we can think of some adjectives for a child like this: brat, control freak, tyrant of the family. Generally speaking, happy is not a word that we would use to describe a child like this. In today's culture, we can tune into any one of our many talk shows and view a show on, "children who bully their parents" or something comparable. What is happening is that this child has too much freedom and doesn't feel safe. He is running helter-skelter in search of the limits. When none are provided, this child feels very frightened and will provoke any adult available to set limits for him. Often when these limits are set, the child feels safe, but this is not what most would observe in this child. What the child might display are angry, defiant kinds of behaviors initially, but with time, this child feels better and safer with the imposed limits.

Another way we can test this hypothesis is to talk to school-aged children. If we ask them what happens in their classroom when they have a substitute teacher, especially a substitute who does not set any limits, children will tell us that some of the kids go wild. Others in the class do not feel safe. We might ask them who they would rather have, their regular teacher or a substitute. Although it might be fun on occasion to have a substitute teacher to test the limits and have a crazy, fun day, children do not want this on a regular basis. It's too upsetting and frightening for all involved. Children do not feel safe without any limits.

There is something else that might happen when a child has too much freedom and does not feel safe. Instead of running wild looking for the limits, the child may become frozen, and withdraw completely. Take another two-year old child placed in a relative's den without adult supervision. Return ten or fifteen minutes later, and we may find this child curled up in a corner crying. The new world of this den is too big, too frightening, too overwhelming. Because this child doesn't feel safe with so much freedom, he withdraws into a smaller space, curling into himself for shelter and safety.

SAFE BUT TOO LITTLE FREEDOM

Now let's look at some examples of people who have learned responsible behaviors to feel safe with freedom, but their freedom is restricted. The first example is parenting a budding pre-adolescent. This child has been taught the rules, has understood the rules and has followed the rules. When given the chance to demonstrate his capability to handle staying home alone for an evening, his parents fear for his safety, so they get a babysitter. The child becomes furious, and a huge screaming battle ensues. This child has the responsible behaviors to handle additional freedom, but his freedom is restricted, so he fights to obtain more freedom.

Another example is one out of the realm of parenting, but one we may be able to relate to personally. An employee, who has worked for an organization for many years and received glowing annual reviews, is suddenly asked to follow the new policy of punching a time clock. The company has installed this device to improve productivity. This employee might get into a verbal battle with her boss or might refuse to follow the new rule or might follow the rule, but decrease her productivity on the job. She had responsible behaviors to handle the freedom she was given but suddenly the freedom has been restricted. She will use powering behaviors, either direct or indirect, to regain the additional freedom. Although she might not use these words, this is what she needs.

To begin to learn how to teach our child self-discipline, we must first understand that self-discipline is related to our genetic instructions for freedom and safety. A child wants as much freedom, choices and options to be able to meet his other basic needs for love and belonging, power, fun and to feel safe. If a child has more freedom than he has responsible behaviors to handle, then he may behave irresponsibly because he does not feel safe. A child may behave in ways that do not meet his own needs or behave in ways that interfere with others' meeting their needs or both. The art of teaching self-discipline is increasing the freedom we give our child as we teach increased responsible and effective behaviors to handle the additional freedom.

NEED FULFILLING ENVIRONMENT

In order for discipline to be taught and learned, we must be teaching in an environment where all involved can meet their needs. If we attempt to follow these ideas in a home where people do not feel loved or where they feel they do not belong or where they feel they have no power, no say in what happens in the home, or where they are not able to have fun or where they do not feel safe, then no disciplinary approach or attempts to teach these ideas will work. Children are ready, willing and able to learn self-discipline and will follow any kind of restriction we place on them as we teach them effective, responsible behaviors if they believe that learning will continue to help them meet their needs. If they believe that they cannot meet their needs, they will continue to behave in an attempt to meet their needs. That may include thwarting our attempts at teaching self-discipline.

Children want to know, "What's in it for me?" If there is more "in it " for them to continue to behave irresponsibly because changing their behavior will mean they get less of what they need and want, then they will be unwilling to learn a different way of behaving. If children learn that there is "more in it" for them by learning responsible behaviors, then they are willing and motivated to learn responsible behaviors, ultimately learning that self-discipline leads to greater need satisfaction.

RULES OF RESPECT

Now that we have set the philosophical and theoretical framework for understanding the "why" of teaching our children self-discipline, let's begin to examine the "how" of this teaching method more carefully.

First, we must establish rules. In order for a child to learn effective, responsible behaviors and feel safe within the freedom of his environment, he needs to know how much freedom there is. Rules establish the balance for safety and freedom. Rules establish limits, helping our child know where his options begin and end. Remember, the genetic instruction for freedom drives us to behave. We want to know how much freedom we have, and we want to know we have enough freedom to meet our other basic needs. We also want to feel safe and not overwhelmed by the options. Rules help our child learn how much freedom he has, feeling safe within the limits and restrictions of the freedom. As our child grows and matures, we are simultaneously teaching increased responsible behaviors, increasing the amount of freedom we allot for our child. As our child learns increasingly responsible behaviors, he feels safe with the increase in his freedom. The rules inform everyone within the home what the limits and opportunities for freedom are.

All rules should follow the general principle of respect: respecting self, respecting others and respecting property. More specifics can be added depending upon the age and stage of our child. The principle of respect enables all to meet their needs without interfering with others' meeting their needs. Using this principle, we have established the framework to help our child learn responsibility.

We must establish our rules through statements of what we want our child to do, rather than what we want our child to stop doing. A rule for a two-year old child may be that chairs are for sitting. So when our child stands in a chair, we can remind him that the rule is that chairs are for sitting and ask our child to sit please. Certainly it would be just as easy to state our rule as "no standing on chairs." However, remember our goal is to help our child learn effective and responsible behaviors to help him follow his genetic instructions to meet his basic needs. So when we state our rules as something we want our child TO DO rather than stop doing, we are simultaneously teaching effective and responsible behaviors. Thus, "sitting in chairs" helps our child learn effective and responsible behaviors better than the rule "no standing in chairs."

Generating and creating rules is an ongoing process. As the adults in the household, we initially have the most input and say as to what the rules will be. As our children grow, needing more freedom, we teach them the responsible behaviors to handle the increased freedom and change the rules, allowing them greater freedom. Everyone in the home is involved in making the rules, giving everyone power.

There are two different kinds of rules: non-negotiable rules and negotiable rules. The non-negotiable rules are those rules that we create and establish. Not every rule will apply to everyone in the family. There may be different rules for different people in the family. If our family consists of more than one child at more than one age, then each child may have a different ability to handle freedom responsibly. Therefore, not all rules are the same for everyone. There may rules that apply to children that do not apply to the adults in the family for the same reasons. Adults, hopefully, will have greater responsible behaviors to handle greater freedom. Certainly there will be some rules that apply to all. (Informing the family when arriving home later than originally planned might be a rule that applies to all, for example.)

NON-NEGOTIABLE RULES

Even if our child does not like or agree with our non-negotiable rules, we still set the limits of the freedom with a non-negotiable rule. As adults, we have more experience of and in the world. Our judgment about what is and is not safe for our child is better. So most of the non-negotiable rules that we establish are to protect our child and keep him safe.

Examples of non-negotiable rules are: always hold a grown-up's hand when walking in a parking lot or crossing the street; wear your bicycle helmet at all times when riding your bike; be home before dark; if you are at a friend's house and then go some place else, call home first so Mom or Dad always knows where you are; all homework must be completed before television watching or playing computer games; always ride with a drug and alcohol-free driver; call home for safe transportation, if necessary; always wear your seat belt; if you are the driver, be sure all your passengers are wearing their seat belts. These examples cover a wide range of ages and stages.

Some non-negotiable rules remain no matter what our child's age or stage; wearing a seat belt is one example. However, what was a non-negotiable rule at one age may change to become a negotiable rule at a later age. Bedtime may be one example. During infancy, our child determined bedtime. During the toddler and pre-school years, we determined bedtime. This continues as a non-negotiable rule during most of our child's childhood. At some point during preadolescence and adolescence, we may turn this matter back to our child as a negotiable rule, with our child negotiating with us what time is best for him to go to bed. Eventually we move to bedtime being completely determined by our child. Changing non-negotiable rules into negotiable ones is based on our child's ability to handle increased freedom because he is learning responsible and effective behaviors to handle this increased freedom.

NEGOTIABLE RULES

We also want to generate other kinds of rules, negotiable rules. This means that we ask all members of the household to help establish rules so that all members of the household can meet their needs, following our general principle of respecting self, others and property. When all members have input in the rules, they also have a greater degree of investment in implementing and following the rules. The ability to help create family rules is an opportunity for all to meet their need for power. By beginning the practice of negotiating rules when our child is very young, we are helping our child learn about rules and what the purpose is for having rules. This helps our child learn principles of self-discipline.

When we begin the activity of establishing family rules with our child when he is young, we will probably do more of the talking than he. Initially there may not be a lot of negotiating for changes on our child's part. It is important to begin asking our child to help establish the family rules early in his life. He is a member of the household, needing an environment where he can meet his needs. His voice is important in establishing what options, opportunities, as well as limits for safety, will help him meet his needs and not interfere with other members of the family from meeting needs. This process continues to be an opportunity to help our child learn responsibility.

As our child grows and matures, he will participate more, offering lively suggestions for rules he thinks are necessary. Because these are the negotiable rules, it is important for us to listen and incorporate our child's suggestions, being sure we also discuss the length of time the new rule will be implemented before we will review and evaluate this new rule. Allowing our child the opportunity for input and implementation of his ideas about the rules helps him follow his genetic instruction for power. Even if the rule seems extreme, as long as it follows the criteria of respect and responsibility, we should implement it, then review and evaluate it fairly soon. The silly or extreme rules will eventually be evaluated out of existence by the family, including by the child who suggested it. Eventually these kinds of rules will stop being suggested. Meanwhile, we have successfully let our child test your sincerity in allowing him to participate and negotiate family rules.

FAMILY MEETINGS

As we have already discussed in Chapter 5, "Creating a Peaceful Place," family meetings are times that the whole family gathers to discuss a variety of things. Included in a family meeting should be periodic review of family rules. (See Table 8, page 149.) The minimum number of times rules should be the agenda item at a family meeting should be at least once a season or four times a year. Discussing rules can certainly happen more frequently as various events and holidays are anticipated. Discussing the expectations as well as rules for special occasions can serve all family members well in participating in the family event, all having clear expectations and guidelines on how they will cooperate together.

Both the non-negotiable rules as well as the negotiable rules should be discussed. Explanations for why a non-negotiable rule exists should be given. The child may voice his opinion at this point, that he would like to negotiate some changes in a non-negotiable rule. A mother can listen to her child's explanation of why he wants a change in the rule, and then she can consider making the changes. If she agrees with his point of view, she may change the non-negotiable rule, either making it a negotiable rule or changing the language of the rule. However, if she believes maintaining the rule as it presently exists is best for the child's freedom and safety needs, she should explain this and stand firm. If there are some kinds of responsible behaviors her child needs to learn before she will consider making a change in the rule, she should explain this to her son as well. Perhaps they can make a plan together to help him learn these behaviors and then discuss the rule change again at a later meeting.

Negotiable rules should also be discussed at the family meeting. This may be the time that parents discuss with their children the change of status of a non-negotiable rule to a negotiable rule. Now Mom and Dad are asking for the children to participate in establishing the limits and the acceptable responsible behaviors necessary for the children to handle their additional freedom.

When my children were three years old, we had a family meeting mid-October to prepare us all for Halloween. At this family meeting we discussed the rules, as well as the final costume decisions. We also included what houses the boys would visit, which parent would accompany them, and what would happen to the sweet treats the boys collected.

When a rule is changed or created, the family should establish when they will have a discussion to review and evaluate this rule. During this follow-up discussion, all should evaluate the success or need for modifications. This may include teaching our children some additional responsible behaviors for handling their additional freedom. Remember, our job is to teach and to insure that our child is learning new effective and responsible behaviors. Planning for further conversations about the rule and our child's ability to handle additional freedom effectively is essential in helping our child be successfully responsible.

Now that Paul and David are licensed drivers, we have had to establish new rules to accommodate this next step of increased freedom and responsibility in our lives. My children have had sixteen years of experience in establishing rules with me, so this latest step toward ultimate freedom and independence may feel large and potentially frightening to me as their mother, but it is not quite so daunting because of the years of practice we have all had.

When parents feel the need to help their child behave effectively and responsibly, new rules can be established at any time. If possible, it is best to bring this up at a family meeting. To explain this, let me give an example from Paul and David's pre-school years. When we would go shopping, usually clothes shopping, they created a game of hiding inside the clothes racks. Although they were having a fun time, I would lose them and often lose my temper as well. So the boys and I created a new rule for how we were all to behave when we went into stores or the bank. Every time from then on, while we were still in the car but about to enter a store, I would ask the boys what the rules for shopping were. After they recited them, I would ask if they thought they could follow the rules today. If they said yes, we would proceed. Upon returning to the car after shopping, I would ask the boys how they did in following the rules. I was asking for their self-evaluation. On those days when they said they thought they could not follow the rules, we would change our plans and not shop. This didn't happen too frequently, but I was relying on their self-evaluations to determine whether or not we could all handle the freedom we were about to face while shopping.

TABLE 8

FAMILY MEETINGS ON RULES

WHEN:
   Fall - Beginning of School Year
   Winter
   Spring
   Summer - Beginning of Summer Vacation

   Anticipating:
      Holiday Time
      Special Occasions or Family Events (vacations)
      New Privileges and Age-related Changes

WHAT:
   Review
      Non-negotiable Rules - what they are
                           - why they exist
      Any non-negotiable rules that have changed to become
         negotiable rules?
      Negotiable Rules
            -What should my changes be?
            - Do any new responsible behaviors need to be learned?
            - When will we review and evaluate the new rule?
WHO:
      Everyone in the family participates in the meeting
      Not everyone in the family has the same rules

NO ONE IS PERFECT

Paul and David, age 11 are in the sixth grade. It is early December, and there has been a snowfall overnight. While all of us are still in bed, we listen to the radio. Finally we all hear the good news that school is delayed because of the weather. Happy with our increased freedom, we all get out of bed for a family breakfast. Following the meal, the boys and I go outside to shovel snow and release cars from their snowed entrapment. While sitting by the fire, warming up with cups of hot chocolate, my husband, Brian, says he is going to get ready to go to work (he is a school teacher, so also had the morning release), planning to leave for work a little early as traveling might be more difficult because of the storm. I realize I am faced with the same potential difficulties, as I am scheduled to consult with a school this day, facing a distance to travel myself. As I rise to go to my bedroom to get dressed I say to the boys, "Don't forget to wear your boots this morning."

"Boots? We're not wearing boots!" David proclaims.

"What do you mean, David?" I ask. "It's snowing outside, and you need to wear your boots."

"No way," David says to me.

I have no patience to discuss this matter with David. Now I have less time to get dressed and travel on the potentially slippery roads.

"David, you and Paul are wearing boots today, and that's it."

"But we'll stay on the sidewalk that we just shoveled," he explains. "We won't get wet feet," he tries to reassure me.

"I don't have time to discuss this now, David," I say, my voice rising and my temper shortening. I also realize I am not going to be around when the boys leave for school, as I will leave before them. "You just better wear your boots or, or, or, I don't know what, but something bad will happen." This kind of threatening behavior is uncharacteristic of me, but I am seeking control of the situation and their health by preventing wet feet. So I turn to threats in an attempt to get my own way. I leave the kitchen, walking to my bedroom, with David right behind me. Paul is right behind David, awaiting the outcome of this confrontation.

"Mom, can we at least talk about this?" David asks in a much calmer tone than is in my voice.

"You can tell me what you think," I say, "but I'm not changing my mind." Even in the midst of this alleged conversation I realize that David is behaving much more maturely than I, but I am running out of time.

David goes on to tell me about how "uncool" wearing boots is, how no other kid on the sixth grade will be wearing them, etc. I only half listen. Finally, I am ready to leave and begin walking downstairs. I realize that I cannot make these children do something they do not want to do. Even if I were going to be present when they left the house for the school bus, I could not wrestle them into boots. I rely on the only ploy left to me. Guilt.

"You're right, David. I can't make you wear your boots. I just hope you do the right thing." These are my final words to my children as I leave for the day.

As I drive to work, I review the scenario in my mind. To add salt to the wound, I am about to present to the school personnel where I am consulting, how to handle discipline differently from threatening and punishing to try and help children to behave the way adults want them to. Luckily, the roads are not treacherous. I realize I have plenty of time and am finally able to see the folly of my behavior and the humor in what had transpired between my son and me that morning.

By noon time, the sun had come out, and all traces of the morning snow melted away. David was right in that prediction.

When I return home that afternoon, both boys greet me at my car.

I begin. "David, I'm sorry about how I treated you this morning. We need to talk about boots and establish some rules now that the winter is coming, but I apologize for yelling and threatening you. It was not a pleasant way for any of us to start the day. Did you wear your boots?"

"That's okay, Mom. No, I didn't," David answers me.

"What about me?" Paul wants to know. "Don't I get an apology, too?"

I couldn't imagine what I had done to offend Paul, but I was more than willing to apologize to him as well, and so I did.

"I wore my boots," Paul explained proudly. "But I didn't have enough room in my backpack for my shoes and my lunch, so I took my lunch out and then had nothing to eat."

Suddenly my apology to him became quite genuine. I took the guilt knife out of my heart, and we all went into the house together.

I share the above story with you for two reasons. The first is that it is much better to establish rules ahead of time, so that when we are faced with varying and difficult situations, everyone has discussed them ahead of time, with everyone being able to discuss what he wants. Based on that discussion, a rule can be established that hopefully all can agree to. The second point of this story is that we do the best we can. I certainly knew better than to threaten, yell and guilt my children into behaving the way I wanted them to, but that's exactly what I did that morning. Even when we have knowledge and good intentions, we will still make mistakes. We must be prepared to understand that teaching self-discipline is a learning process, not just for our child, but also for us. We must accept the possibility of our own mistakes, and apologize when we make them.

MAGIC

When our child misbehaves, he is attempting to get something that he wants to follow his genetic instructions. From the child's perspective, not having what he wants is the problem. From the parent's perspective, the child is behaving against the rules, something that the parent does not want. When we understand that our child is behaving to get something that he wants, then we can quickly move into the role of teacher, helping our child learn more effective behaviors to help him get what he wants and do it in a way that allows him to follow the rules.

The next time our child misbehaves or behaves in a way that is against the rules, let's first ask our child, "What are you doing? Please stop." We should use a neutral tone of voice. This statement is a reminder for our child to stop and think about what it is he is doing, to evaluate if it is against the rules. In asking this question, we are asking our child to stop, think and self-evaluate.

If our child continues to misbehave, then ask the magical question: "What is it that you want that you are trying to get by _____?" Fill in the blank with whatever the misbehavior is that our child is doing. It might be pinching. Then the question would be, "Sally, what is it you want that you are trying to get by pinching your brother?" This is the same question as asking our child "why" he is behaving so. If we have ever asked children "why" they are behaving they way they are, we will be familiar with the two ways that children most frequently answer this question: "I don't know," or "He did it to me first." Neither answer is satisfactory or helpful. The magical question asks essentially for the same information, but because it is framed in an understanding that all behavior is purposeful, there is a slight twist to the question.

We know why children behave because we know why all people behave. People behave to get something that they want that will help them follow their genetic instructions. When a child misbehaves or behaves in a way that is against the rules, his motivation is the same. He is behaving to get something that he wants to follow his genetic instructions. When we ask the question phrased this way, children know the answer and share it with us.

"Sally, what is it you want that you are pinching your brother to try to get?" Sally may tell us that she wants to color with the marker that her brother has. Then we ask, "If we can help you figure out a way to get the marker and still follow the rules, are you interested in learning?" From a great deal of experience, my own as well as other people's who have used this magic, I can assure you that Sally and every other child will answer "yes." Children do not want to misbehave just for the fun of it. Their behavior is purposeful. They don't know a better, more effective and responsible way to get what they want. They are doing the best they can, which in fact may be against the rules. Our job, as the adult and parent, is to help our child get what it is he wants and to help him learn how to do this responsibly, within the rules. It really is magic! (See Table 9, page 154.)

TABLE 9

MAGIC
*ONLY PROGRESS AS FAR AS YOU NEED TO *

STOP- THINK- SELF-EVALUATE

1. What are you doing? Would you please stop.

MAKE A PLAN TO LEARN RESPONSIBLE & EFFECTIVE BEHAVIORS

2. What is it you want that you are trying to get by hitting?
   - A. Are you willing to figure out another way to get what you want without hitting?
   - B. Together make a plan to help child get what he wants and follow the rules.
   - C. Follow-up conference

RESTRICT FREEDOM

3. Time Out
   - A. Only as long as it takes to teach child responsible behaviors to get what he wants effectively
   - B. Only in the area where he bas demonstrated he has more freedom than he has responsible behaviors.
   - C. Make a plan to re-instate freedom. Include follow-up conference.

NEED

4. Is there some need the child is not able to meet successfully at this time?
   - A. Ask child.
   - B. Make a plan; include follow-up conference.

FOLLOW-UP CONFERENCE
DECREASE FREEDOM
Ask child to self-evaluate: "How did you do following our plan?"
"Are you now able to get what you want and still follow the rules?"

Sometimes a child's behavior is potentially harmful to himself or someone else, so we need to do more than engage in a conversation as described above. We become aware that our child has more freedom than he has responsible behaviors to handle because we observe his behavior. In these situations we may need to use "time out" to decrease his freedom temporarily. However, in these situations we should only time our child out for as long as it takes for him to learn the responsible behaviors to regain his freedom. We should only "time out" or restrict freedom in the area where our child has demonstrated that he has more freedom than he can handle and where he needs to learn more effective and responsible behaviors to handle this freedom.

In other words, if our child is having a food fight at the dinner table, we need to restrict his freedom at the dinner table. Threatening to take his freedom away after dinner, telling him that if he doesn't start behaving with some manners, there will be no television after dinner doesn't make sense. Our child has not demonstrated by his behavior that television watching is an activity with too much freedom. What he is demonstrating is that today he doesn't have the responsible behaviors to sit at the dinner table. Let's see how this process would look:

Matthew, age seven, started playing hockey with his green peas and knife. He was asked what he was doing, then asked to please stop. This game stopped but was followed by his getting ready to pass his brother the salt as if throwing a forward pass on the football field. His mother has asked Matt to please leave the table, sit in the den in what has been designated by the family as a "time out" chair. After just a few minutes, Matt's mother goes into the den to have a conversation with Matt about dinner.

"Matthew, what is it you wanted that you were trying to get by throwing the salt to your brother instead of passing the salt?" Matt's mom asks him.

"I wanted to have some fun at dinner. I hate what Dad made for dinner. I wasn't having any fun eating it,

so I thought I could make some different fun," Matthew honestly answers.

"Matt, was throwing the salt against the rules?"

"Yeah," Matt answers.

"If we can figure out a way for you to have fun at dinner and still follow the rules are you interested?" Matt's mother asks.

"Yeah, I guess," Matthew answers. "But how can I have fun at dinner if I don't like what Dad cooked and I still have to follow the rules?"

"I don't know either," his mother answers. "I have two suggestions for you, though. One, you can sit here until you come up with an idea, then call me and we can discuss it. You're a very creative kid, Matthew. You seem to be able to have fun anywhere you are. Or the other idea I have is that you can come back to the table, join the family, and we can all come up with ideas. But if you come back to the table, you have to be willing to follow the rules of how we eat together. What do you want to do?"

"How about if I sit here for awhile and see if I can come up with something myself. If I don't have any ideas, or if I want to come back to the table, I will. But I'll only come back if I think I can do it and still follow the rules."

"Sounds like a plan, my man," Matt's mom agrees.

🏠　　🏠　　🏠　　🏠

Clearly, Matthew was not getting what he wanted to meet his need for fun while simply sitting at the table faced with a dinner he didn't enjoy. So he was behaving to meet his need for fun. The problem was that his behavior was against the rules (not respecting others or property) and interfered with other people's meeting their needs. After he had been asked once to follow the rules and he demonstrated through his behavior that he still was not able to meet his needs and follow the rules, his mother determined that Matthew had more freedom than he had responsible behaviors to handle. So she asked Matt to decrease his freedom by moving to the "time

out" spot. Matt's freedom restriction was not for a predetermined period of time. He stayed in time out for as long as
he needed to learn the responsible behavior to resume his
freedom, including the behavior of deciding he could follow
the rules. His mother talked with him about the purpose of his
"misbehavior" and helped Matthew determine some alternative
ways to meet his needs and still follow the rules.

This evening, however, Matt may have been better able to
meet his needs by staying in the den by himself and fantasizing
all the fun he could create at the dinner table. When dinner was
over, if Mathew still had not returned to join the family, he
would be allowed to leave his time out place. In fact, even
before dinner was over, Matt could have talked with his mother
about leaving the time out place. Together they probably could
have worked out other things that Matt could do to meet his
need for fun. But he could not return to the dinner table
without first making a commitment that he would follow the
rules. Tonight might have been a night where Matthew was
better nourished through play and fantasy than food.

When using "time out," we must understand that what we
are doing is temporarily restricting the freedom of our child
because through the child's demonstrated behavior he has also
demonstrated that he has more freedom than he has responsible
behaviors to handle. We restrict the freedom while simultaneously using the magical questions to help determine what it
is our child wants. Then we quickly help our child learn the responsible, effective behaviors to get what he wants that still
follow the rules. With that accomplished, we quickly reinstate
the restricted freedom. There is no specific duration for "time
out." The amount of time is determined by the child's willingness to learn an alternative way to get what he wants and
still follow the rules. Freedom is only restricted in the area
where the child has demonstrated that he does not have effective, responsible behaviors.

After we have reinstated our child's freedom, armed with a
plan for behaving responsibly, we must engage in a follow-up
conversation with our child. This does not have to be a long
exchange. We ask our child for his self-evaluation of how he is
now handling his freedom. Has the plan of behaving responsibly helped him to get what he wants? If not, we make a

better plan. We share with him our assessment of his successful ability to get what he wants and follow the rules.

In the story at the beginning of this chapter where Paul and David used the hose in the sandbox, freedom was restricted only in the area where they needed to learn more effective, responsible behaviors. Their misbehavior did not affect their permission to have dessert after lunch. Cookies and hoses were not related to one another. Trying to help a child learn to behave differently, more responsibly, through restriction and pain doesn't make sense.

In reviewing this story I can see some things that I would have done differently. Once the boys demonstrated that the running water and a sandbox were too much of a tempting combination the first time, I should have moved the hose or shut off the water strongly enough that their tiny hands couldn't have gotten them into trouble. But once again, I was doing the best I could and what made sense to me at the time.

LOOK TO THE NEEDS

All behavior is purposeful. The purpose of all behavior is to help our child get what he wants to satisfy one or more of his needs. We have asked our child the purpose of his behavior, have made a plan to help him learn new effective and responsible behaviors to get what he wants, and yet he continues to misbehave. Although we are looking for the magic, it is eluding us. What now?

If our child continues to behave irresponsibly, perhaps what he says he wants, what he is telling us he wants, is only partially satisfying to one of his genetic needs. Instead of wanting something, he may be needing something. However, even he is unaware of what that may be.

If we have diligently followed the process of peaceful discipline as outlined and we find that we and our child continue to engage in correcting or issues of his misbehavior, we should begin investigating our child's ability to meet all of his needs effectively. Does he feel safe and secure? Is he feeling loved and able to belong? Is he feeling powerful and able to feel recognized? Is he laughing and having fun? Does he feel he has options and is able to make choices? Spend some time thinking about answers to these questions. Have a conversation with your child and ask him for his answers.

When my children were toddlers, I found I was spending a great deal of my interactions with my son, David, correcting his behavior, asking him what he wanted that he was misbehaving to try to get. It felt as if most of our interactions with one another were around my correcting him or monitoring his behavior. I thought about what all his behaviors had in common. I thought about how he was meeting his needs. What I guessed was that David was not feeling satisfied with the love and belonging from and with me. The next day, with new resolve, I spent increased time with David, asking him to read a story with me, go for an adventure walk with me in the yard, eat his snack with me. Suddenly his continuous misbehaving stopped. What David needed was a greater sense of connection with me. All his previous behavior had been an attempt to satisfy this need. When I helped him meet this need and get more of what he wanted, more of me, he no longer needed to misbehave.

If after discussing and investigating, we discover that our child is not able to meet one or more of his needs effectively, we should make a plan to help him. We have not lost the magic but need to understand that he needs something he is not getting.

AN ONGOING PROCESS

Paul and David, age 11, are sixth graders. They have a day off from school and are playing at a friend's house for the afternoon. When I answer the telephone, Paul is on the other end.

"Mom, can we go to a movie?" he asks.

"Who are you going with, what are you going to see, who's driving you there and back, whose money will you use?" I ask the litany of questions that I need answered before I can give the boys the permission for the increased freedom they are requesting.

"I'll call you back," he answers. Not long after, I get another call from Paul. "We're going to see 'Curly Sue.' If you drive us there, the Smiths will pick us up. We'll pay using our own money." All sounds fine to me, and I

tell him so. A little while later Paul calls again, informing me that the Smiths are willing to drive in both directions. He tells me what time I can expect the boys to return that evening. When they come home at their designated time I ask how they enjoyed the movie. Both give me a non-specific negative answer.

The next evening while I am preparing dinner, Paul asks if he can speak with me in my office. I agree, wondering what is up. Usually when one of the boys wants a conference in the office, it means they either have a personal hygiene question or want to complain to me about something their father has done. When we are settled in the office, Paul says, "We didn't go to see 'Curly Sue' yesterday. We went to see 'Friday the 13th'." This was a movie they both knew I would not have given them permission to see, as it was rated over their age unless accompanied by an adult. We had also discussed these kinds of horror movies, and they knew I did not want them to see these kinds of films.

"We need to talk about this," I say. "I appreciate your telling me the truth. I'll fill your father in. Does David know that you were going to tell me this?" When Paul made his confession, he was also tattling on his brother.

"No," Paul answers. "But I'll tell him now."

I intentionally eavesdrop on Paul's conversation with David. "Good," David replies when Paul tells him what he has told me. "If you hadn't told her, I was going to."

When I speak with Brian about what Paul has confessed to, I emphasize our needing to praise the boys about telling us the truth. We both realize that the boys are of an age where they are away from us more frequently. There are going to be lots of opportunities for them to make bad choices now, and we want them to feel safe enough and confident enough in how we work things out with them, so that they will tell us about the mistakes they were making, rather than trying to hide things and get into difficulties that may be more than they can handle on their own.

David requests that we hold off having this discussion until after dinner is over so that he won't be upset while he is eating. We honor this reasonable request.

"Boys, you know what you did was against the rules, right?" Both nod their heads. "Neither your father nor I am glad you did what you did, but we are very glad that you told us about it. How did you manage to get into the movie?" I ask.

"Mr. Smith drove us and stayed with us," David answers. "We told him you had given us permission."

I made a quick decision not to deal with the lying, thinking that lying is a behavior that the boys used to get what they wanted. Lying is a purposeful behavior as well. What my husband and I are most concerned about at this preadolescent age is that they will eventually tell us the truth and ask for our help and support when they make bad choices, helping them learn how to make better choices without our immediate supervision and immediate guidance.

"Did you enjoy the movie?" I ask.

"No, it was terrible," Paul answers. "It was more stupid than scary."

"So I wonder if there should be a consequence since you deliberately broke a rule. What kind of consequence do you think is fair?" I ask.

After several minutes none of us is able to think of any. Paul finally says, "Maybe we shouldn't be allowed to go to any movies for another month."

"But you only go to the movies about once a month," I answer.

"Maybe there shouldn't be any consequence this time," Brian suggests. "Seems as though you made a bad choice, but you came and talked with us about it instead of trying to hide or lie to us any further. Maybe we should just say we all learned what we needed to from this situation."

We all agree that is the best thing to do. The next time the boys ask for permission to go to a movie, however, I am more diligent in my monitoring what they were going to see and are they sure that is the movie

they really intend to see. A small amount of trust has
been lost and needs to be regained.

I tell the above story to emphasize once again that teaching
our children self-discipline is an ongoing process. This
teaching process continues for the child's childhood until he
reaches the age of adulthood. There is no hard and fast way to
approach the very important and ongoing issue of self-discipline. Flexibility is crucial for both parents as well as for
children. Both children and parents are learning self-discipline.

SUMMARY

• Teaching self-discipline is an art, not a science. We are
learning and practicing our art of peaceful parenting. Our
children are learning the art of self-discipline.

• Responsibility means meeting our needs in ways that do
not interfere with other people's meeting their needs. This is
an external value or moral. Children are born driven to follow
their genetic instructions. They are not born knowing how to
follow their instructions responsibly.

• Children must learn how to meet their needs responsibly. We are the teachers and guides for our children as
they are learning effective and responsible behaviors.
Parents should expect that children will misbehave and make
mistakes as part of the learning process.

• Teaching responsibility means balancing freedom needs
with safety and security needs. When children have too much
freedom they do not feel safe. When children have too little
freedom, they may feel safe but restricted. Too much
freedom or too little freedom can lead to poor behavioral
choices.

• The art of teaching self-discipline is slowly increasing the
child's freedom while teaching him the responsible behaviors
to handle the increased freedom.

• Teaching self-discipline will only work in an environment
where people believe they can meet their needs. Children will
learn self-discipline if they believe that learning will increase

need satisfaction. If children believe that they cannot meet their needs by learning self-discipline, then they will continue to misbehave in an attempt to meet their needs.

- The family must establish rules. Rules inform everyone of the boundaries for safety as well as the limits to freedom. Rules should follow the principle of respect: respect self, respect others, respect property. The principle of respect establishes the definition for responsibility.

- Non-negotiable rules and negotiable rules should exist in the family. Allowing all members of the family to participate in creating the negotiable rules helps to satisfy everyone's need for power. Creating the rules is part of the process that helps our children learn responsibility, leading to self-discipline.

- At least four times a year or once a season, family meetings should include a discussion of the rules. Additional meetings anticipating special events and holidays, where expectations and rule discussion can also help these occasions, run more smoothly and are more need-satisfying for everyone.

- A child's misbehavior is not the child's problem. Not getting what the child wants is the child's problem. Asking our child what he wants that he is trying to get by misbehaving is the magical question that will help us teach our child effective and responsible behaviors to get what he wants and follow rules.

- If a child demonstrates through his misbehavior that he has more freedom than he has responsible behaviors to handle, we should decrease the child's freedom. Freedom restriction should only be in the area where the child has demonstrated he has too much freedom. Freedom restriction should only be as long as it takes for us and our child to plan for responsible behaviors to re-instate the freedom.

- If we have followed the practice of peaceful discipline, and our child continues the same kinds of misbehavior, we should investigate our child's ability to meet his needs. His misbehavior may indicate his inability to meet his needs.

- Teaching and learning self-discipline is an ongoing, life-long process. No one is perfect, neither our child nor us. We must expect and accept mistakes as part of the process of learning self-discipline.

Chapter Nine
Behavior is not the Problem; it is the Language

BEHAVIOR IS LANGUAGE

We have already discussed the idea that behavior is a person's best attempt, acting in the real world, to get what is wanted in the quality world to satisfy one or more of the basic genetic needs. This was discussed at length in Chapter 3. In the last chapter we discussed the idea further, from the point of view of a parent who may be dealing with a child whose behavior is against the house rules or interfering with other people's ability to meet their needs in the home. In this chapter we will again be discussing behaviors, but now we will be looking at behavior as the language used to communicate quality world wants and desire for need satisfaction. Sometimes this form of communication is verbal, but we can understand ALL behavior as a form of communication or language communicated in code. To help us understand this idea of behavior as a form of language, let's investigate a parenting story.

FRUSTRATION MEANS "I WANT SOMETHING I'M NOT GETTING"

Karen, a married professional nurse, works evenings and alternating weekends so that she and her husband can share the responsibility of parenting their three-year old son, Bobby. They have arranged their schedules so that one of them is always home with Bobby, using no outside child care.

After attending an introductory lecture I gave explaining the instructions our children are born with,

Karen became increasingly aware of problems she was experiencing as a mom. Following one activity where Karen was asked to chart her level of desire for the basic needs, her level of effort at attempting to meet these needs and her level of satisfaction in meeting these needs, Karen became acutely aware that her needs for freedom and fun were severely lacking. She was aware of her frustration that turned anger to rage because she was not getting what she wanted. Karen was also acutely aware of the ineffectiveness of these behaviors.

Usually her days spent with her son began the frustrating exchange. "I had planned a fun morning. My son and I would attend a play group where he could play with his friends. Instead of his cooperating with me by helping me to dress him, he would fight with me, wriggling and struggling against me as I tried to put on his shirt, his pants, his shoes. I knew I was engaging in short-sighted controlling behaviors with him. But it felt like if I stopped trying to put on his shoe, then he would feel he won, feel an increase in power, and the next time he would struggle even more. I felt that consistency and clear communication would lead me to greater personal control and power over my son's actions. So I would hold down his leg and put on his shoes. If that didn't work, I would continue to increase the force of my movements until he gave up the struggle. My perception of the struggle was that he was dissatisfied with my mothering skills. I thought that he did not like my choices for activities each day and was physically rejecting me. The perception of rejection tainted my view of reality and turned the struggle over shoes into a struggle for acceptance."

🏠   🏠   🏠   🏠

At this point Karen is aware that she is not getting what she wants in her relationship with Bobby. She is also guessing that Bobby is also not getting what he wants. Karen's awareness of the problem is good, but like many of us, she is viewing Bobby's behavior as the problem. To a certain extent she is correct. From her perspective of what she wants, which is

Bobby's cooperation in helping him dress for the day's activities, his behavior is the problem. Luckily, Karen did not stop her investigation there.

QUALITY WORLD INVESTIGATION

WHAT DO I WANT?

"In my quality world there are harmony and peace, love and cooperation within the family at all times. We would always work together for the common goals dictated by me. I would prioritize the goals to fit my perception of our community needs. For instance, we would visit people whom my son and I both enjoyed. The subsequent group would include another mother-toddler combination. In my quality world, my son appreciates the thought and effort I make toward satisfying his needs. He would cooperate enthusiastically with the plans I've made and would say, "Mommy you're awesome! I really love and appreciate you." And I would respond, "I love you, too. You're awesome, too. What a team we make."

🏠   🏠   🏠   🏠

Although Karen is aware that her quality world is not realistic, this does not keep her from wishing and dreaming of her ideal family situation. Luckily, she does not stop to censor her investigation of her quality world with worry about whether or not she can realistically ever achieve her quality world picture. Courageously exploring her quality world picture of a family and her power and control in the family leads her to an ultimately clearer assessment of the problem between herself and Bobby.

WHAT DOES HE WANT?

"My son's quality world is quite different from mine. It consists of Mom's undivided attention, positive regard and unconditional love 24 hours a day. He wants me to

be an interactive toy, cuddly blanket and magician who can effortlessly make all his favorite foods appear. In his quality world, he dictates when it will be sunny and where and with whom he will play. He would never have to take a bath, never brush his teeth and eat whatever he wants whenever he wants it."

🏠   🏠   🏠   🏠

Although Karen doesn't know for certain that this is Bobby's quality world picture, it certainly sounds typical of the behaviors, demands and requests of a toddler. There may be some pieces or parts of the picture that Karen is not aware of. Because she is relating to her son, age three, she is smart to rely on her best guess because at this point he has only limited verbal language to communicate with her about his quality world pictures. She is viewing his behavior as the language he uses to communicate what he wants and needs in the world, including what he wants and needs from her.

BEHAVIOR COMMUNICATES A NEED

"When I reviewed the morning struggle of dressing from a basic needs perspective, I realized I was expressing my need for power first. I was attempting to use this power to achieve the end of fun and freedom which will ultimately lead to a strong sense of belonging and love."

🏠   🏠   🏠   🏠

By looking at herself from a basic need perspective, Karen is beginning to increase her self-understanding. Using powering behaviors to meet the need for freedom is not very effective. Karen is beginning to understand how her behavior, although the most effective available to her at the time of confrontation with Bobby is ultimately not the most effective in helping her get what she needs.

🏠   🏠   🏠   🏠

"My son is expressing his need for freedom and power over his own body. These are first and foremost

in his mind. He seems to have no concept of the future fulfillment of his other basic needs. Only the present need is of importance to him."

🏠　　　🏠　　　🏠　　　🏠

By watching Bobby's behavior carefully, Karen is beginning to recognize what needs Bobby is attempting to meet. His behavior, although a problem for her because it is interfering with her getting what she wants, is not the problem. Bobby's behavior is the language he is using to express what it is that he needs. As is true for a toddler, he is not concerned about the future. His focus is on getting what he needs right now, in the present moment.

WHAT WE BOTH NEED AND WANT

"After reviewing our interactions from this perspective, I decided to move our quality worlds closer together to try to create opportunities for Bobby to meet his needs in a different way. I decided to change my approach toward getting him dressed every day. I began to pretend that there were elephants in his pants and lions in his shoes that needed to be kicked out so that Bobby could get his legs and feet in. At first, Bobby was surprised by the change, but soon he caught onto the game. He was meeting his need for fun by playing the game, and he felt a greater sense of power because he was controlling the imaginary animals. After he was dressed, I gave him a big hug and said, 'Thank you. I appreciate that, Bobby.' That was my attempt to help him feel love and belonging with me. It also allowed me to feel love and belonging toward him. This changed our whole morning routine. We are both now able to meet our need for love and belonging with each other. With his cooperation I feel more freedom, and he feels more fun."

🏠　　　🏠　　　🏠　　　🏠

What a great idea! Karen used her own vivid imagination to tap into her son's basic needs for fun and power. He was able to work with her, thus feeling connected to her, and able to have fun at the same time. Bobby was able to meet his need for powering over the imaginary animals in a playful, fun way. Karen was able to meet her need for connectedness in finding a playful way for her son to cooperate with her in accomplishing the daily task of getting Bobby dressed. Now their day could begin with fun, power and connectedness, giving both of them a greater sense of freedom.

SUCCESS BREEDS SUCCESS

"With that success I decided to approach another issue, hoping both of us could meet our basic needs by combining our quality world pictures. Every suggestion that either my husband or I made to Bobby was turning into a battle. So one morning I sat down with him while he was eating breakfast and said, "Bobby, Daddy and I have noticed that you want more control over your life. For instance, we notice that you want to have control over when you get dressed in the morning. How can we help you with this?" Bobby enthusiastically helped me make a list of six categories where he could have more control of his daily routine and successful completion of tasks. These included getting dressed, helping to brush his teeth and take a bath as well as washing hands and face before and after meals, choosing which toys to take in the car with him, helping to cook and being allowed to complete a quick project before needing to leave for daily activities. Initially our plan was to give Bobby a sticker for each successful task completed. After a certain number of stickers had been accumulated, he would earn a surprise. Much to my surprise, however, he earned so many stickers so quickly that I suggested to him we do away with the stickers. This was okay with him. What he wanted was to direct and have more control for himself during our day."

As was the case for Karen, success often leads to more success. Her willingness to consider working differently with her son in other areas of their life resulted from her successfully learning to listen to what her son's behavior was communicating to her. She was also tuning in more carefully to her own language of frustration and anger as a means of communicating with herself that she was not getting what she wanted.

Because Karen understood Bobby's battling and uncooperative behavior as a message he was sending to her, she correctly understood that he was demanding and fighting to have greater power and control in his life. Good for Bobby! That is just what most toddlers are working towards, as we already discussed in our overview of ages and stages in Chapter 6. Karen correctly viewed her parental responsibility as providing more opportunities for Bobby to meet his need for power. Instead of continuing in the pattern of Bobby fighting with her and her husband for power throughout the course of their days together, Karen worked with Bobby to develop a plan where he could increase his power. Karen was happy and willing to work with Bobby in defining areas where she could provide greater opportunities for him to follow his power instruction.

MEETING NEEDS IS REWARD ENOUGH

Although Karen initially believed that she would have to provide some external reward for his successfully completing tasks, eventually Karen learned that Bobby's ability to increase his power need during the course of the day was reward enough for him. Karen did not need to provide some outside incentive. Luckily, Karen was still tuned into Bobby's behavior as language and stopped externally rewarding his cooperation. If she had continued giving stickers that would lead to a prize, what she might have discovered is that Bobby might stop cooperating. A child's withholding cooperation in following a plan may be because receiving rewards interferes with his ability to feel powerful. Instead of feeling powerful, some people feel manipulated with rewards, quite the opposite of powerful. Bobby was following the plan he and his mother made because the plan helped him to follow his genetic instructions to meet his basic needs. He felt an increase in power and control because the plan allowed opportunities for him to be in charge in certain areas of his life. He felt a greater sense of love, belonging and cooperation with his parents because they were all working together to accomplish daily tasks and chores. He did these things because they gave him an internal good feeling and sense of satisfaction. Bobby's motivation came from inside of himself. No external reward or additional incentive was needed.

BEHAVIOR IS NOT THE CHILD'S PROBLEM

"Much to my amazement and delight, both Bobby and I were more successfully able to meet all of our needs. I discovered that what I thought was my greater need for freedom was corrected by increasing the options and freedom for my son. Increasing his freedom and power opportunities helped me more successfully meet my needs for freedom and fun. Ultimately I think we both feel a greater sense of love and belonging with each other, as each day now begins with our working, laughing and playing together."

🏠   🏠   🏠   🏠

Karen and Bobby were able to work out how to increase their need satisfaction with each other because Karen was willing to approach her own as well as Bobby's behavior courageously as the language to communicate what they both wanted. Although initially Karen viewed Bobby's behavior as the problem, she was able to consider his behavior from another point of view. Bobby's behavior was HER problem, because his behavior was interfering with her getting what she wanted and needed. Bobby was not doing anything TO her, although that is how it felt. Bobby's was behaving FOR himself. Karen's judgment of Bobby's behavior as uncooperative was Karen's behavior to help her get what she wanted. Luckily she was able to evaluate the ineffectiveness of her judging behavior. When Karen reviewed what she wanted, she was then able to begin asking herself questions about what Bobby might want. This enabled her to realize that Bobby's behavior was the language he was using to tell her what he wanted and needed. For Bobby, not getting what he needed and wanted was the problem.

When we are presented with situations in our day where we criticize or judge another's behavior, we have an opportunity to change our perspective and evaluation. Instead of deciding that the other person's behavior is the problem, we can realize that this other person is doing the best she knows to get what she wants and to follow her genetic instructions. Our upset and negative judgment usually comes from our belief or fear that this other person's behavior will keep us from getting what we want and interfere with our own ability to follow our genetic instructions. If we can increase our own awareness of what we want in this situation, then we can begin to ask ourselves what the other's behavior might be communicating to us about her wants. We then have a greater chance of working successfully with the other, so we can both get what we want and follow our genetic instructions without interfering with each other.

The next time our five-year old nags and argues with us during our weekly grocery shop or the next time our 12-year old screams about how unfair our stupid rules are or the next time our 14-month old repeatedly awakes in the middle of the night asking for water, we begin to consider this as their form of language to us about wanting something they are not getting. Although we may continue to criticize and negatively label our child's behavior, consider that our unhappiness about our child's behavior is also an indication that we may not be getting what we want in these situations. We ask ourselves what we want and then guess or ask our child what she wants. We see if we can figure out a way, asking our child's help, how we can both get what we want and meet our needs cooperatively. Although it might feel as if our child's uncooperative behavior is the problem, remember, it is our child's best attempt to follow her genetic instructions. This behavior is a language that we can learn to decipher to work with our child so that we are both able to get what we both want.

LYING

Although this may be difficult for some parents to believe, lying is not our child's problem. Our child uses the behavior of lying when she is not getting something that she wants. She believes that lying is the most effective behavior available to her to help her get what she wants.

Lying is a problem, but for the parent. Many parents have a belief or picture in their quality world that includes their child's being truthful. So when a child lies, the problem is the parents.

All behavior is purposeful, including the behavior of lying. The purpose of all behavior is to help individuals meet their basic need and follow their genetic instructions to get something that is wanted in their quality world. So, lying is a behavior that our child may use to get something that she wants to satisfy a basic need.

There are times in the age and stage of our child's life where lying may be a more frequent occurrence. During a child's young life, from two to four years of age, our child may use "magical thinking" that an adult may interpret as lying. "How did this vase get broken?" a mother may ask her toddler. "A monster came in, stomping his feet and shook the vase onto the ground," may be her reply. Adults may think of this behavior as lying. But what our daughter is doing is creating an explanation that gets her off the hook and keeps her mother approving of her, something that she wants. So this behavior is purposeful in helping her get what she needs and wants, a continuing loving relationship with her mother.

During a later stage of pre-adolescence and adolescence, a child may lie to do what she wants to do that she has been specifically told not to. She wants to keep from getting into trouble. She wants both her freedom and her connected relationship with her parents. "Did your parents give you permission to go to the mall?" the father of our daughter's friend asks as he drops the girls off for the afternoon. "Oh, she won't mind," our daughter answers, knowing full well that we have told her not to go to the mall to hang out. Our daughter wants the freedom of frequenting a place that her friend is allowed to go even though this is something we do not want. She lies to her friend's father so she can get what she wants.

I do not mean to say that lying is a behavior that parents should accept from their children; I am saying that lying is a behavior that parents can expect from their children. Lying is a purposeful and sometimes effective behavior that all people, including our child, use to help them get what they want.

There are many religious as well as ethical and philosophical explorations of lying. The ninth of the Ten Commandments, "Do not bear false witness against your neighbor," is one example. Among the challenges that we parents face is the difficult task of teaching our children that "honesty is the best policy," only to be challenged by our eight-year old when she overhears us declining an invitation to a party we do not wish to attend, by lying. Many a parent has been embarrassed by the brash honesty of their three-year old when she forthrightly and loudly shares her observation of a "fat lady over there" in the grocery store.

I do not mean to make light of the difficult job parents face in teaching our children this moral or value. I am simply trying to point out a new understanding of how and why we do the things we do, including lying. Lying, as a behavior, is not the problem. It is the language.

Knowing and expecting that our child may lie to us at some point during our lives together, I am suggesting an additional means of handling this challenge. First, we must investigate and fully understand the picture we have in our quality world of our child as being an honest person. Is that a picture for us? Why? What are the reasons that we believe and want our child to be honest? Are there times when we believe lying is more harmful than other times, or are we of the belief that lying is ALWAYS wrong? I do not mean to say that there is one right answer to these questions. Rather, I am asking us to understand our own positions better, our own right answers to these questions, through personal self-reflection.

Once we have fully understood our own quality world picture about honesty, then we are in a better position to work with our child when, and if, she lies. We now know that WE have a problem when our child lies. Our problem is that we want our child to be honest, and she is not being so. Now, we need to find out what it is that our child wants that she is attempting to get by lying? Is it that she wants to go to the mall even though we don't want her there?

As we have already discussed earlier in this chapter and in the last, now that we know what our child wants and we have shared what we want, we can work with our child to see if there is some way that our child can get what she wants without needing to lie to us. Again, I do not mean to imply that there is always a way for this to happen. Perhaps no matter how much our daughter wants to hang out at the mall, we still will not give her permission to do so, but attempting to help our child learn how to get what she wants without lying will increase the chances that our child will stop lying.

Children often lie because they fear the negative consequences or punishment by telling the truth. If we eliminate the negative consequences (grounding, taking away privileges), we have increased the probability that our child will be honest with us.

When my children reached pre-adolescence, my husband and I were diligent about keeping open our communications with our children. We wanted the boys to feel free to tell us all of the triumphs and difficulties they faced in their daily lives. This very conscious decision was based on the belief that the boys would be facing greater challenges and choices in their lives. We wanted them to feel free to talk with us so we could help them continue to learn effective behaviors in dealing with all the choices and challenges that they faced in their lives as they emerged into adulthood. Included in our conversation with the boys was the possibility that they could lie to us to avoid negative consequences from us because of our potential disapproval. However, we have reassured them that if they come to us with a problem, we will do our best not to punish them, but rather to help them solve the bigger problem. We explained that lying was a behavior they might use to help them get what they want. We would rather help them get what they want without needing to lie. This was the decision my husband and I came to through our own reflection of honesty, based on the pictures in our quality worlds. This may not fit for you. I encourage you to spend time thinking about honesty for yourself, as well as for your child.

Finally, let me also share that, as a child, I was a liar. I was very good at it, usually able to fool my parents, sisters and friends. My mother was aware of my lying and was quite upset and baffled by it. She and I had many a conversation about the hazards (the boy who cried wolf story) and difficulties of lying. Usually the conversation would end by my lying to my mother, telling her I would never lie again.

Eventually I decided to give up lying. I decided for myself that the bad feelings I had about myself inside felt worse than any humiliation or punishment I could receive from telling the truth in the moment. I eventually decided that lying, although effective in the short run, was ineffective in my feeling good about myself in the long run. Lying was a behavior that helped me get some of my quality world wants, but ultimately I realized that lying kept me from maintaining my quality world picture of who I ultimately wanted to be.

SUMMARY

• Behavior is the language a person uses to communicate her quality world wants for need satisfaction to herself and to the world.

• Either our own or our child's negative feelings, like frustration, anger or upset, are the language indicating that a person wants something she is not getting.

• We need to take time to investigate fully our quality world picture of what we want and our child's quality world picture of what she wants. If our child is too young to verbalize her desires, guess, based on our knowledge of the basic genetic instructions our child is born with, as well as our knowledge of our child's age and stage. When investigating quality world wants, we should not censor what is not realistic or possible. Our logical mind may believe our wants are unrealistic or improbable, but that doesn't keep us from wanting it.

• Based on our new understanding of what we want (and need), and what our child wants (and needs), we can develop a strategy that will allow us both to get what we want and need. This may mean modifying our quality world picture, or it may mean finding the similar pieces of our two quality worlds. We should aim our effective behaviors toward the combined quality world picture.

• Since behavior is the language our child is using to communicate to herself and the world what she wants, our job as parents is to help our child learn more effective behaviors to get what she wants.

• Behavior is not our child's problem. Not getting what she wants is our child's problem. Her behavior, because it is different from our quality world picture, is our problem.

Teaching our child effective and acceptable behaviors to get what she wants solves both of our problems.

• When our child learns effective behaviors to get what she wants, she is intrinsically rewarded and satisfied. No external reward is necessary. In fact, providing an external reward can be counter-productive.

• Lying is a parent's problem and a child's behavior to try to get something she wants. Children often lie because they fear the consequence of telling the truth. Eliminating this consequence, while simultaneously teaching our child effective and acceptable behaviors to get what she wants without lying, help solve both of our problems.

Chapter Ten
Criticism - A
Destructive Habit

The family of five is seated for the evening meal. All members of this family know that the chances are very good that sometime during the course of this meal, the middle child, Cheryl, will spill her milk. What happens next is equally predictable. The father, Hank, will shout, criticizing the child for what she did wrong causing her to spill the milk. This sensitive child will become so upset by the incident that she will flee the table, seeking the sanctuary of her room. Those remaining at the table will be equally upset but will try to continue the family meal. Another family meal ending in explosive anger is anticipated by all before they sit down to eat together.

HOPED FOR CHANGES

How could this family scene change? There certainly are many alternatives that would help this situation. The first might be to change the kind of glass or cup the child is drinking from. Another alternative might be to fill the container a little less full. Another might be to discuss with the child ahead of time what solutions she thinks might be best to help her avoid spilling her milk. A previous discussion would probably need to include determining whether or not the child wants to find a way to get through her dinner without spilling her milk. A further solution might be that the child doesn't drink her milk at the table, but instead leaves the table to stand alone by a counter, where there are fewer obstacles to distract her and contribute to her spilling the milk. I'm sure there are additional options that are not even listed here.

The least desirable option would be to continue the scene, night after night, where this child's father criticizes her for spilling her milk with the hope that this form of correction will produce a different result. Although he directs his criticism at only one child, all other members of the family are also affected by the upset, including the father.

Before too many of you begin to criticize me for pointing out the error of the father's ways, let me quickly state that I realize that this father had the best of intentions in mind. He was not interested in lowering his child's self-esteem or in belittling her. What he wanted was what the rest of the family wanted. That was to enjoy family time while they ate a meal together as they all shared with each other their day's events and activities. He hoped that by correcting his daughter through criticism she would learn a better way.

CONSEQUENCES OF CRITICISM

The problem is that criticism, even when it appears to work, has profoundly negative consequences. When it does change the immediate behavior, the price paid for changing another person's behavior through criticism may be a damaged relationship. Sometimes it is the relationship between critic and the person being criticized. Sometimes it is the relationship the criticized person has with himself. Either way, it is a heavy price to pay for results that can be attained by other, more loving and productive ways.

Through this book we have been thinking about people and behavior from a different perspective. Now we can think about better ways to handle difficult situations. Offering more effective options to help change another person's behavior, if the other person has evaluated that there is a need to change his behavior, may work. Using the vital tool of self-evaluation, something already built into each person's system, can have very positive results.

SELF-EVALUATION

Here is how using this idea would work. First, the father, Hank, needs to evaluate the effectiveness of his own behavior. In order to evaluate, he must have something to evaluate against. Initially Hank needs to spend some time exploring his own quality world picture of what he wants at the family meal. Let's assume his answer would be something along the lines of wanting a pleasant, reasonably spill-free dinner with his family. Next he needs to ask himself what he is doing to get what he wants. If he is being honest, included in his list of behaviors would be his reaction when his daughter spills her milk. When his daughter, Cheryl, spills her milk, Hank yells and screams at her. Now he can ask himself if yelling and screaming are working to help him enjoy the kind of family meal that he wants. At this point the ineffectiveness of his own behavior will be as apparent to him as it is to us.

What is it Hank is hoping yelling and screaming will produce? Probably his answer will be "helping Cheryl learn to not spill her milk at dinner." Now we have helped him to decipher the two specific wants in his quality world picture. Hank wants the family meal to be pleasant for everyone in the family. He also wants to help his daughter learn how to eat a meal and manage herself and her food. Hopefully Hank does not expect that every meal will be completely spill-free, as accidents happen, no matter what a person's age. Hopefully he is now more willing to accept that his job, as the parent, is to help his daughter learn effective behaviors to decrease the possibility of accidents occurring.

Hank is now aware that what he is doing is not working to get either of the things he wants. He also is aware that if he behaves as the teaching parent to help his daughter learn more effective ways to drink her milk without spilling, then he will get the pleasant family meal he wants. As the adult, he can learn more effective ways, different from yelling, to help him get what he wants. As the parent, his job is to help his daughter learn without criticizing her.

TEACHING A BETTER WAY USING SELF-EVALUATION

Instead of Hank's trying to teach his daughter through criticism, he is ready to help her learn using the same process he has used for himself. Long before the family meal, Hank sits with Cheryl and asks her for her quality world picture of the family meal. At the same time, he shares with her his quality world picture of the family meal. Both are pleased to learn the similarities and differences in their quality world pictures. Hank listens as Cheryl tells him how she looks forward to this time because it is the time she gets to brag to him about all the things she has done during the day. Hank tells Cheryl how he looks forward to that time to find out all that is happening during her days when he is not with her. They both talk about this time as being a very important time for love and belonging with everyone in the family.

Next Hank asks Cheryl what kinds of things she is already doing to help the meal match her ideal picture. At this point he adds additional behaviors he has observed in his daughter that contribute to the successful match between what they both want and what the actual dinner experience is like. This is also the time to add spilling milk to the list of behaviors. Although this is a difficult and sore topic for both of them to discuss, because they have spent time together talking with each other about their quality world pictures of the family meal, chances are good that Cheryl will be willing to add milk spilling to the list of her behaviors.

Hank shares all his own behaviors to have the kind of successful family dinner he wants as well. He also includes his shouting, yelling and criticizing. He asks Cheryl if there are other things she is aware of that he does during dinner that he did not list.

Now Hank is ready to ask Cheryl to self-evaluate her behavior at dinner, as well as to self-evaluate his own behavior. He may go first, telling Cheryl what things he is doing that he feels match both of their pictures of what they want the meal to be like. He asks Cheryl to do the same, that is, list those things that she is doing that she feels are matching the family meal quality world picture they have already discussed. He also needs to tell Cheryl what behaviors he thinks he needs to change in order for their meal together to be more like what they both want. Again he asks Cheryl to also share those behaviors she thinks she needs to change in order to have a successful family meal together.

Chances are very good that both he and Cheryl are willing and anxious to discuss behaving differently. Because neither has been shamed or blamed about their ineffective behavior, both are ready to work together to figure out more effective ways to behave at the family meal even when things are different from their wish.

Again Hank goes first. "When I yell and scream at the meal, Cheryl, it is because I want to help you learn a better way to drink your milk without spilling. I realize that yelling has not helped you learn. Can you help me figure out a better way to behave, if you or anybody else spills something during dinner?"

"Yes," Cheryl is quick to help her father learn a better way. "You could say 'Oops, we better clean this up' like my teacher does at school when we spill things."

"Great idea," Hank says. "But sometimes I lose my temper before I have a chance to say that. Could you help me by saying the 'Oops' part first? Then you could look at me and say 'And what do you say, Daddy?' I think that would help me remember that I am going to say, 'We better clean this up' next." Cheryl smiles in agreement. Together, they have now helped Hank work out a better way to behave at the table so that the meal is more like what they both want.

Now it's Cheryl's turn. "Cheryl, is there a plan that you and I can figure out to keep you from spilling your milk? I don't mean always because accidents do happen. But perhaps we could work out something so that we decrease the chance that you might spill your milk. Are you willing to do that with me?"

Cheryl nods her head yes. She is willing to cooperate to change things because both of them have had difficulties, and both of them are working on a plan.

"Any ideas, Cheryl?" Hank asks.

"When I sit down for dinner, I get so excited, I have so much to say, and I get so thirsty. Maybe if I drink some milk before we all sit down together that would help, but Mommy has told me not to fill up on milk before dinner because then I'm not hungry for dinner." Hmm, Hank can see part of the dilemma his daughter is caught in.

"I have an idea, Cheryl," Hank says. "How about if we give you only a little bit of milk just before dinner. We'll check with Mom to see if she thinks that's okay. Then when we fill your glass at supper, we'll still only give a small amount. If you want more, we will keep filling it, but only a little bit at a time. That way, when you drink, even though you're excited, there will be less milk in the glass so it might be less likely to spill." Cheryl smiles and nods her agreement. "How about if we try that at tonight's dinner and see how we make out?" Hank asks.

UNWILLINGNESS TO SELF-EVALUATE

Let's take this scene down a different path, one where Cheryl is less cooperative. Just as was described above, Hank still meets with Cheryl at a time well removed from meal time. As was described before, he begins by discussing with Cheryl his quality world picture of what the family meal would be like, asking her to do the same. This time Cheryl is not willing to volunteer her own ideas. This needn't stop Hank. He still shares with Cheryl what he hopes their time together can be like, why he has these ideas and that he ultimately hopes family meal time can be a pleasant and loving experience for everyone in the family.

Hank can still share with Cheryl all the things he is aware of that he is doing to lead the family meal in his hoped for direction. Included are his yelling and shouting at her. Now would be a great time for him to apologize to her for his unkind behavior. He can again explain that what he wants is to help her learn to eat with the family without spilling and that he yells to help him get this. He admits that he realizes that this is not helpful to her and not helping him have the kind of family meal that he wants. He can ask Cheryl to add any other behaviors that she is aware of that Hank does during dinner.

Whether she adds to his list or not, Hank can still self-evaluate in front of Cheryl that he thinks he needs to change some of the things he is doing at dinner to lead in a more positive, successful direction. At this point he once again asks Cheryl to help him brainstorm some alternatives to his shouting and yelling. Certainly, if she has any suggestions, he can incorporate them into his plan. "You can stop yelling and shouting at me," Cheryl offers. Although this is not an alternative behavior, rather is a suggestion for stopping a behavior, Hank will increase his success of Cheryl participating with him if he acknowledges and incorporates what Cheryl says. "Yes, I will stop yelling and shouting. Instead I will immediately stand up, get the sponge and paper towels and say to you 'Let's clean this up.' I will do my best to be kind and helpful to you Cheryl. I do not want to criticize or hurt your feelings any more. Spilled milk can be fixed, and right now I am trying to fix the hurt and upset between us." Hank is being very clear about what he wants, what he has been doing that has not been working, what he will do differently in the future, and how he wants to heal the hurt and upset between he and his daughter to improve their ultimate relationship.

Although Cheryl has not actively participated in the process this time, Hank needs to continue to meet with Cheryl regularly, reviewing his own progress in changing their family dinners. He continues to ask her what she wants of their meal. Eventually when Cheryl sees her father change as he committed to doing, she may begin to trust that he wants to help her to move in the direction of a pleasant and loving family meal together. This may take time, but Hank is willing to do the work because he wants to heal the division between himself and his daughter that criticism created.

CRITICISM STOPS LEARNING

Instead of verbally criticizing, shaming and blaming as a way to help both father and daughter have the kind of family meal they both want, utilizing self-evaluation, where father self-evaluates his own behavior and then helps his daughter to self-evaluate her behavior is not only more pleasant and more peaceful, it also then becomes a lesson in problem solving, a skill that children need to learn and practice during childhood and well beyond. (See Table 10, page 186.)

Exploration and learning about oneself and the world is a major function and job of childhood. As parents, our job is to help our child learn and explore. Part of what occurs during this exploration and learning is children making mistakes and errors. As parents we should expect that this will happen. In fact, this is an expected step in anyone's learning process. The first time we play a musical instrument errors and mistakes may occur. This is a normal part of the learning process. When anyone is faced with criticism while exploring, learning shuts down.

However, as an adult, it is very difficult to be around someone who is doing things incorrectly, especially if that someone is our own child. We often feel tempted to step in and correct. Part of our job as parents is to correct. The trick is learning how to correct while allowing our child to maintain his natural curiosity and desire to explore. Using the built-in system of self-evaluation allows both to be maintained: our desire to correct and the child's curiosity and desire to explore.

We, as the parents, must also learn to balance intervening and correcting with leaving our child alone to discover on his own, including making mistakes. Errors lead to learning and discovery, too. Many an invention and innovation came from mistakes!

TABLE 10

STOP CRITICIZING, START SELF-EVALUATING

What do I want that I am trying to get by criticizing?

Is criticizing helping?

Is criticizing effective?

What else can I do to get what I want without criticizing?

Would it help to include my child in this planning?

Would it help to improve my relationship with my child if I apologized?

Would it help to ask my child to self-evaluate and make a plan, too?

CORRECTION

Obviously, there is no hard and fast rule about when to step in and correct and when not to. (See Table 11, page 187.) Safety is an obvious guideline that can be used. When my two-year old children were playing near our coal stove while I had temporarily stepped out of the room, I was not concerned with correction, criticism or self-exploration as I grabbed them and quickly moved them away from the danger of a burning stove. Afterward, when they were safe, we had a conversation about what they had done and why playing on the bricks was out of bounds. (The coal stove sits on a platform of bricks in our family room.) During this incident, safety was paramount, not worrying about technique.

Most of the time, however, imminent danger is not an issue. Creating an ever-expanding safe place as our child grows and matures in which our child can follow the natural inborn instruction to explore and discover is our job as parents. This includes discovering when a mistake has been made, discovering what the mistake leads to and learning what steps to take to correct a mistake.

There is so much in the world that is new to our child. Expecting correct, mistake-proof behaviors is unreasonable, unrealistic and an error on the part of a parent. Learning when it is time to intervene and correct and when to back away and allow our children their own discovery of errors and mistakes, is part of what makes the job of parenting an art.

When young, my children used the expression "on accident" to describe when something happened that was not intended. "I kicked his leg on accident when I went to kick the soccer ball," would be a typical statement from one of them in explaining to me why his brother was crying. I thought this a clever creation as I was sure it developed from the alternative possibility of one kicking his brother on purpose. Eventually I did correct them, explaining that the common expression is "by accident". Now we humorously share the expression "on accident" purposely. The correction was a simple statement of what is commonly said without any judgmental expression of the words they were using.

TABLE 11

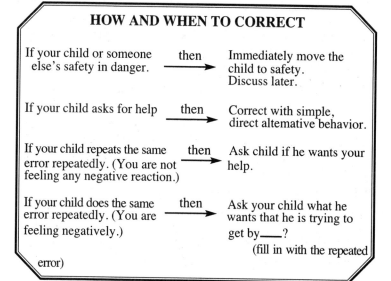

HOW AND WHEN TO CORRECT

If your child or someone else's safety in danger.	then →	Immediately move the child to safety. Discuss later.
If your child asks for help	then →	Correct with simple, direct alternative behavior.
If your child repeats the same error repeatedly. (You are not feeling any negative reaction.)	then →	Ask child if he wants your help.
If your child does the same error repeatedly. (You are feeling negatively.)	then →	Ask your child what he wants that he is trying to get by____? (fill in with the repeated error)

SIMPLE, DIRECT STATMENT

The key to correction is simply stating what change in beha-vior the parent is looking for. A toddler standing on the chair can be corrected with "Sit please". There is no need to point out what the child is doing wrong although initially we may want to remind our child that "In our home we sit in chairs." There is no need to count the number of times our child has been corrected within the last hour. There is no need to criticize or judge that your child's mistake or error is a reflection of anything other than his lack of experience of the world.

ALL BEHAVIOR IS PURPOSEFUL

If the child's mistaken behavior persists after we have simply provided an alternative corrected behavior, then it's time to remember that all behavior is purposeful. Although more subtle, continuous correction is a form of criticism as well. When our six-year old interrupts the conversation between us and our visiting aunt for the ninth time in the course of a 30-minute conversation, our job as the parent is to remember that our child is behaving in a purposeful way. He is interrupting in an attempt to get something that he wants, driven by his basic needs. There is no need to criticize our child in front of our aunt attempting to save face. Instead, we should turn to our child and ask "What is it that you want that you are interrupting to try to get?" If our child has no answer, then we can guess that he probably wants to be part of the conversation or at the least wants our undivided attention for a few moments, just as we are giving such attention to our aunt. Criticizing our child, either in the moment or later, will not help either one. We may feel as if criticism will work, but remember, the change in the behavior will only be temporary and may certainly affect our relationship with our child or our child's own feelings about himself.

CRITICIZING OR CONTINUOUS CORRECTION IS A CLUE

Correction is necessary when helping our child learn and grow to become a part of this world. Too much continuous cor-recting can turn into criticism. Criticism, although a parent's immediate attempt to help to correct and increase learning in a child, becomes defeating and destructive. Continuous criticism, no matter how well intentioned, may result in a child with poor self-esteem and may hamper or destroy the relationship between critical parent and the child. As a parent, if we notice that we are continuously correcting or criticizing our child, we can take that as a clue that we need to spend some time in self-exploration. What is it that we want that we are attempting to get through continuous correction or criticism? Our criticizing behavior is purposeful. We are using the behavior of criticizing to get something that we want. Remember that criticism is not an effective behavior. Taking the time to discover what it is that we want will help us learn and plan more effective behaviors that will not destroy our relationship with our child.

SUMMARY

- When we criticize our child, we do so hoping to correct or change our child's behavior. The intention of criticism generally is the hope it will correct our child's mistake or error.
- Consequences of criticism may be a temporary change in our child's behavior, but it may also damage our child's relationship with us or our child's feelings about himself (self-esteem).
- Self-evaluation is the process that is much more productive and effective in helping our child change his behavior. Self-evaluation is an inherent part of each person's internal process.
- When our child has self-evaluated that his behavior is not effective in getting him what he wants, our child is ready and willing to learn a more effective, alternative behavior.
- When our child is unwilling to self-evaluate and learn a more effective alternative behavior, we need to increase our involvement and improve our relationship with our child. Apologizing for criticism begins to heal the damage between us. We can also self-evaluate what we were hoping for when we criticized our child. Sharing with our child our plan for implementing a more effective plan to help us get what we want may help our child learn the process of self-evaluating.

- When a person feels criticized or is repeatedly corrected, learning and curiosity stop.
- When we correct our child, we should simply state the alternative behavior we want in a neutral or friendly tone of voice.
- All behavior is purposeful, including the behavior of criticizing. If we find we are criticizing or continuously correcting our child, take that as a cue to take some time for ourselves. We need to ask ourselves what we want that we are trying to get by criticizing.

Chapter Eleven
Looking Back on What's Ahead

CHOICES AND CONSEQUENCES

Most parents are interested in being the best parents they can be. Some set out on their path of parenting, vowing to do things differently from their own parents. From personal experience, they are aware of the damage and upset that can result from some parenting practices. Others are determined to do as good a job as their own parents. Still others do things just like their own parents, without conscious awareness, more or less on automatic pilot. The purpose of this book is not to imply that some perfect form of parenting exists. Rather, the purpose of this book is to help parents do the best job of parenting they can, asking parents to be aware of the choices they make as parents.

No matter what parenting choices we make, there will be other choices and options we do not make. For instance, in a two-parent household, if both parents work outside of the home, then this family has not made the choice to have one parent remain a stay-at-home parent. We simply cannot make both of these choices simultaneously.

With each choice made, there are also consequences. When a parent makes a choice to remain a stay-at-home parent, there are consequences associated with this choice. Any parenting choice has consequences that affect the entire family.

If we set out to parent differently from our own parents in an attempt to avoid certain obstacles or consequences, there will still be consequences. Perhaps these consequences will be different, but there will be consequences nonetheless. Whatever the choices we make, there is also no guarantee that these choices will be perfect. We can prepare ourselves for better parenting choices, with the accompanying consequences if we stay conscious of the choices we make.

Throughout this book I have encouraged each parent to become aware of the genetic instructions he is born with and that his child is born with. The consequence of choosing to understand and follow these instructions is greater happiness, satisfaction and success for the parent and child. The daily consequence is greater personal harmony and peace as well as increased peace and harmony between a parent and his child. When we understand our own internal motivations as well as the motivations of our child, we are more likely to develop strong, satisfying relationships with one another. Not only does this help with the relationship between parent and child, but also with all other relationships in our lives. Certainly teaching these concepts to our child increases her ability to develop additional relationships in her life.

Just as it is possible to assemble a holiday toy or birthday gift without following the enclosed instructions, it is also possible to do the same as a parent. Some assemblers will be intuitively successful as they build a structure without following directions, no matter how many parts or how complicated the process. Others may build what appears to be a successful assembly, but will have parts left over. Hoping for the best, the child is presented with the toy. Some withstand the child's play, but others fall apart.

Rather than hoping for the best or relying on intuition, this book sets out to help parents decipher and understand the instructions that each child is born with. The consequence of choosing to parent peacefully means that parents follow the guidance that their child's instructions provide. Helping our child learn her own instructions provides her with a solid foundation for living. As a parent, we do not have to worry about leftover parts compromising the foundations that our parenting provides. During the difficult and challenging times of our lives and our child's life, our child will not fall apart because she understands her own genetic instructions. She will have learned effective behaviors that will lead to her satisfaction while maintaining quality relationships with other people, all contributing to her strong, capable mental health.

SHIFTING PERSPECTIVES

This book views human behavior from a different perspective. Many people believe, because of their own observations, as well as traditional educational information, that we live in a cause-effect world. That is, people do the things they do because something happens outside of the person causing the person to behave. For instance, when driving, we stop at an intersection because a traffic light turns red, or we answer a telephone because it is ringing.

Throughout this book I have tried to explain human behavior differently. People do the things that they do because of their own internal urges arising from their genetic instructions. Although an observer may believe that a red traffic signal stops a driver, our new understanding of human behavior helps us to understand that the reason a person stops at a red traffic light is because the person wants to live through the intersection. The person's internal motivation or quality world picture of continued life generates her stopping behavior.

With the advent of telephone answering machines and services, we can better understand the motivation for answering or not answering a ringing telephone. We do not answer or ignore a telephone just because it rings. We decide to answer the phone or not because we either want to speak with the person who is calling or we do not. There are a wide variety of reasons that people choose not to answer a ringing telephone: they spend their day at work on the phone, so they want the evening phone free; the activity they are currently engaged in is more interesting or important then whatever the telephone is beckoning for; they know who is on the other end and don't want to speak with them, etc. Answering machines inform us how best to behave to match our quality world picture with the person calling us on the telephone. The latest invention of caller-ID, where the identity of the person calling can be known even before we answer the phone, determining the subsequent answering or not of the ringing telephone, further helps us to understand that all behavior is internally motivated.

With this understanding, we could better explain animal behavior as well, although that is clearly not the focus of this book. The classic experiment that proved it was the external ringing of a bell that caused a dog to salivate would have been substantially changed had the experimenter opened the dog's cage. Do you think the dog would have waited for the bell to ring or do you think the dog would have run for its freedom?

As humans we do the things we do because of our genetic instructions. We receive information in the world that helps us determine how we will behave to help us get what we want to satisfy our physical and psychological needs. So the red traffic signal and the ringing telephone are just information. Neither of these things causes any person to do anything. It is a person's need-satisfying quality world pictures that cause her to do something or not do it. Some people stop at red traffic signals, but some people do not. Some people answer ringing telephones, but some people, even with no answering machine, do not answer the phone every time it rings.

Shifting our understanding of human behavior to a different perspective around issues of stopping at traffic lights or answering ringing telephones is relatively simple. However, this shift may be more challenging when it involves the more critical issues of raising and relating to our children. Some may think that, not only is it a challenge to think about our child's behavior differently, but many of the ideas and suggestions in this book are too difficult to follow. Who has the time and the focused energy to follow what I have outlined for peaceful parenting? Why should I even try?

ANOTHER SHIFT

During the last few years, there has been a good deal of attention focused on describing and investigating the "dysfunctional family." Our country seems obsessed with understanding and then excusing some behaviors due to the dysfunctional family system. Where are the guidance and information helping us to understand what is involved in creating a functional family?

The view of human beings and human behavior as dysfunctional is a tradition that was established with the advent of modern psychology. It began with Dr. Sigmund Freud, a physician who studied then described human psychology using a biological and medical model. This was revolutionary, as previously people with psychological difficulties were described as evil and possessed by the devil. Freud viewed human beings as being either neurotic or psychotic. He failed to describe a healthy person, however. Most of Freud's work was done with people who were having difficulties functioning effectively in their lives. People who were able to cope and handle their daily lives did not seek the counsel and help of Freud.

Abraham Maslow, a psychologist, changed this tradition. He believed that there was much to be learned about human beings and human behavior by investigating healthy people, people who were able to lead effective and satisfying lives. As a result of Maslow's work, he suggested that all humans are born with basic needs, from the need to survive to the need to become self-actualized. Although the needs that Maslow described are somewhat different than those I have presented in this book, his work shifted the view of human life from a deficiency or disease perspective to a perspective describing healthy coping, as well as people's desire to strive for excellence.

As we have already discussed, our brain functions as a negative feedback loop. That is, we receive an urge to behave when we view the world as being different from what it is that we want. When the world matches our hoped for quality world picture, we may feel satisfied and comfortable, but there is no accompanying urge to behave. So there are times that we may overlook things when they are the way we want them. With this understanding, it is easier to understand why psychologists might have first researched and sought to understand what was happening for individuals who had difficulties handling their life. Unhealthy individuals stood out, driving researchers to understand their difficulties and seek solutions. But researching and understanding healthy and functional human beings makes eminently more sense. These people who have their own solutions to their own problems are our teachers.

More recently, there has been a change in focus to understand systems better, not just individuals. Considerable research has investigated dysfunctional and deficient systems that contribute to human failure and upset. Depending on which researcher we read, we may learn a wide variety of contributing factors leading to this dysfunction, both society's as well as the families'.

However, most recently, there has been increased research and investigation of resiliency. Why are some people with similar high risk factors, including similar family and societal challenges, able to "rise above" their difficulties and become successful, effective, functioning members of society, and others are not? In other words, there has been an increase in research, shifting from a deficiency model to a competency model. The results describe resiliency, an adaptive human behavior that enables some people to overcome and cope with difficulties, no matter how impossible the adversity seems.

Resiliency is the ability to bounce back, recover from or adjust to misfortune or changes. Research has revealed certain factors leading to a child's resiliency. The three strongest factors contributing to a child's resiliency are: a sense of humor and ability to have fun (the need for fun); a sense of detachment or healthy distancing from the disorganizing or dysfunctional element or person in the family (the need for freedom); the presence of one healthy adult (the need for love and belonging). (Burns, 1994) The research also describes protective factors for resiliency: a sense of control (power) and a sense of bonding (love). (Burns, 1994) Although the research does not outline the genetic instructions in the same format as I, the information is consistent. Interestingly, in the resiliency research, the need for love and belonging is mentioned twice. Certainly in terms of importance, the need for love and belonging is worth mentioning twice.

WHY PEACEFUL PARENTING?

Information and guidance to help parents create functioning families, as well as providing strategies to foster resiliency in our children does exist. I hope this book will contribute to that information as well.

"The solution of adult problems tomorrow depends upon the way we raise our children today. There is no

greater insight into the future than recognizing when we save our children, we save ourselves."
Margaret Mead

Consciously choosing how we will parent takes time and effort. Peaceful parenting is a job that mandates focused energy and determined resolve. But as the above quotation from Margaret Mead reveals, our future depends on how we teach and treat our children today.

Although some may say that to follow the guidance of this book takes too much effort and work, I would ask where better to place our efforts? Daily happiness and satisfaction do take energy and work. The future of our child, as well as the entire planet, depends upon parents' willingness to expend the daily energy and effort necessary to help raise our children, humanity's future.

The initial effort and work to understand our own instructions as well as our children's will subside once we have begun thinking this way for awhile. The first few weeks and months will be more difficult, however, because we are going against what we have come to believe is "the way things are." Anytime we learn anything new, it feels awkward and difficult. This shift of thinking is no different. However, once we begin to move in the direction of noticing our own internal instructions and begin to work with our child's genetic instructions, our learning will have progressed. We will discover that all the work and effort are worthwhile. Our changed thinking and new view of ourselves and our child will become more familiar. We will eventually see that approaching our lives and our parenting job this way is easier, less time consuming and less of a struggle. Along the way we will feel the internal good feeling that comes from learning anything new.

Addressing one parenting area as a specific example may help explain this point. It is easier and quicker to correct our child's "misbehavior" by swatting her behind. In fact, this method is effective the first few times we use it. But as some of us may know from personal experience, eventually this type of correction stops working. Our child persists in "misbehaving" and may learn that hitting is something acceptable in her home. Parents are then faced with a dilemma. Do they increase the strength of the spanking, hoping that inflicting more pain will work more effectively to change the child's behavior? If not, then what else can they do?

Following the process of teaching our child self-discipline, as I have described in Chapter 8, "Peaceful Disciplining," takes much more effort, time and work initially. However, parents who choose to assist their child using this method, understanding that the child's behavior is her best attempt to get what she wants, that she doesn't know a more effective way of getting what she needs except through the "misbehavior," discover that the increased time, effort and work eventually shift to less time, less effort and no work. Eventually the child learns self-discipline. She may time herself out when necessary. She will ask her parent to help her learn more effective ways to get what she needs and wants before she "misbehaves." Peaceful parenting means that we work with our child to help her learn how to work with us. All of the work, effort and time we put in, pays off with feelings of pleasure, pride and satisfaction. We feel good as a parent because we see the fruits of our labor as our child matures and grows into a happy, effective human being. The adage of "anything of value takes time and effort" is accurate when describing the job of parenting. Do any of us have a job that is more important?

WISHES AND GIFTS

I have never specifically touched on any spiritual or religious ideas and ideals throughout this book. I realize that sharing such information would be based on my quality world pictures. My effort has been to describe a process for parents so that each could clarify and understand his own quality world pictures and beliefs. However, I will share some of my thoughts as I reach the end of this book.

Children are the most precious gifts a parent will ever receive. Watching and participating in the unfolding of another human being is an ongoing and remarkable miracle. Our child begins life so vulnerable and unprepared, yet hopeful and receptive to all we have to give and teach. This tiny person eventually matures into an adult who is capable, strong and independent. Awesome! The unexpected gifts we encounter along the way include the discoveries we make about this emerging human being, as well as all the things we learn about ourselves.

Not only are we receiving our child as a most precious gift, we are a gift to our child. Some of us may believe, as I do, that it is not just biology that connects parent and child. Our children may have been given to us because of what they have to teach us and what we have to teach them. Our unique relationship with each other holds unexpected lessons that only we can provide for each other.

Our child is remarkably lucky because we are her gifted parent. Remember that, as we receive our gift of this child, she is also receiving her gift: us as her parent.

Some children are not as lucky as our children. They do not have parents who are able to love and care for them. All children deserve to be loved, respected and honored as miraculous gifts to the world. The charge of all adults is to treat all children with the love, respect and honor they deserve, so they can evolve and emerge, capable of bringing to the world whatever individual and unique possibilities they carry within them. I encourage all of us, as humans who care for and care about children, to reach out to these children who are not as fortunate as our own in whatever capacity we can.

When I wish upon a star, one of my wishes is that all people will see their job as parents as the first and most important priority in their lives. I wish all people will better understand themselves and their children as nature intended. I wish that some day all people will use the ideas and strategies Mother Nature provided for us.

Finally, I wish us all luck. As I began this book, I discussed the good luck I had, receiving the love, support and wisdom of my own parents. I have also been remarkably lucky to parent two amazing and wonderful sons. Perhaps none of this was luck, but a little bit of luck can help all of us as we live together on this planet. I wish us luck, love and the strength and courage it takes for us to build peace together.

SUMMARY

- Every choice results in consequences. No matter what parenting choice we make, there will be consequences. We will be better parents if we make conscious choices.
- The consequence of choosing to parent peacefully is greater happiness, satisfaction and success for both parent and child. This also leads to a satisfying relationship between parent and child, as well as satisfying relationships with others.
- The purpose of this book is to help parents decipher and understand the instructions their child is born with. This provides guidance for the parent and for the child, building a solid foundation for living.
- This book asks the reader to shift thinking from a cause-effect world to understanding that people are internally motivated and that all behavior is purposeful.
- Recent research describing and defining resiliency in children found that fun, freedom, love and power contribute to a child's resiliency capacity.
- Peaceful parenting provides strategies to foster resilient children and help to develop functioning families.
- Peaceful parenting takes time, effort and work, especially in the beginning. As a parent and child are better able to understand themselves, ultimately it takes less time, less effort and less work. Where else is our time, effort and energy better spent than in parenting?
- Children are a parent's greatest gift. Parents are a child's greatest gift. Not all children are as lucky as our own. Reach out to love, honor and respect all children, helping them to grow and provide for the planet the unique contributions they are here to give.

Burns, E.T. *From Risk to Resiliency*. Dallas, Texas: The Marco Polo Group, 1994.

Thanks to Alex Bogle for the title of this chapter.

References

Boffey, D. B. *Reinventing Yourself*. Chapel Hill: New View Publications, 1993.

Burns, E. T. *From Risk to Resilience: A Journey with Heart for our Children, our Future*. Dallas, TX: The Marco Polo Group, 1994.

Dawson, B. C. *The Solution group: Positive Change through the group Process*. Chapel Hill: New View Publications,1993.

Glasser, W. *Reality Therapy*. New York: Harper & Row, 1965.

Glasser, W. *Schools without Failure*. New York: Harper & Row, 1969.

Glasser, W. *Positive Addiction*. New York: Harper & Row, 1976.

Glasser, W. *Control Theory*. New York: Harper & Row, 1984.

Glasser, W. *Control Theory in the Classroom*. New York: Harper & Row, 1986.

Glasser, W. *Quality Schools*. New York: Harper, Collins, 1992.

Good, E. P. *In Pursuit of Happiness: Knowing what you Want, Getting what you Need*. Chapel Hill: New View Publications, 1987

Good, E. P. *Helping Kids help Themselves*. Chapel Hill: New View Publications, 1992.

Kohn, A. *Punished by Rewards: The Trouble with Gold Stars, Incentive Plans, A's, Praise, and other Bribes*. Boston: Houghton Mifflin Company, 1993.

Powers, W. T. *Behavior: The Control of Perception*. New York: Aldine De Gruyter, 1973.

Sullo, R. A. *Teach Them to be Happy*. Chapel Hill: New View Publications, 1989.

Peaceful Parenting
PO Box 271
Portsmouth RI 02871
www.peacefulparenting.com

Index